D1377503

Are We There Yet?

Are We There Yet?

ROBERT L. MILLET

DESERET
BOOK
SALT LAKE CITY, UTAH

DESERET BOOK is a registered trademark of Deseret Book Company.

Visit us at deseretbook.com

Library of Congress Cataloging-in-Publication Data

Millet, Robert L.
  Are we there yet? / Robert L. Millet.
      p.   cm.
  Includes bibliographical references and index.
  ISBN 1-59038-436-9 (hardbound : alk. paper)
  1. Christian life—Mormon authors.   2. Spiritual formation.   I. Title.
  BX8656.M53   2005
  248.4—dc22   2005002458

Printed in the United States of America   72076
Publishers Printing, Salt Lake City, Utah

10   9   8   7   6   5   4   3   2

To Richard L. Chapple—
treasured friend, beloved mentor, dynamic leader,
a true Latter-day Saint whose gospel gladness
and optimism continue to inspire

True doctrine, understood,
changes attitudes and behavior.

—BOYD K. PACKER

Contents

CONTENTS

Introduction

DURING THE YEARS THAT WE lived in Tallahassee, Florida, our family would drive to Louisiana to visit my folks a couple of times per year and to Utah to see Shauna's folks whenever we could. Both seemed long and tedious trips, especially with a car full of children. We would listen to tapes, read stories, sing, and play games, all in an effort to make the time pass more quickly and to draw attention away from the fact that we still had a formidable drive ahead of us. While the journey to Louisiana wasn't bad, the drive to Utah was a backbreaker in more ways than one. We didn't have a lot of money, so occasionally Shauna and I would attempt to "drive straight through," that is, make the forty-hour drive without stopping overnight at a motel along the way.

Inevitably, the kids would ask at least twenty times during the journey: "Are we there yet?" or "How long until we get there?" or "Are we *ever* gonna get there?" As parents, Shauna and I would try to be patient, assuring them that indeed this trip would eventually come to an end and before long we could get out of the car and enjoy life again. Because we had made the trip many times, we could be quite precise about the time of arrival. We could tell them what cities and towns and truck stops and vacation sites were ahead. When the children would complain that we would *never* get to Baton Rouge or Salt Lake City, we could dutifully say, "Now come on. Of course we're going to get there. Look at the map and find where we are now. See how far we've come already? Isn't that exciting?"

The years have come and gone, and those young children are now grownups, some of them with children of their own who ask on family vacations, "Are we there yet?" I suppose that our children explain to their children what's going on, where they are, and how much longer the ordeal will continue, much as we did.

Life's a lot like that. It's not uncommon to ask ourselves, "Are we there yet?" or "Is my life where it ought to be?" or "Is my course in life pleasing to the Lord?" or "If I died now, would I obtain eternal life hereafter?" These are important questions. They point us toward things that matter most. We have been told that eternal life is the greatest of all the gifts of God (D&C

6:13; 14:7), so it's perfectly reasonable to want to know of our standing before the Almighty.

As we consider where we are in relation to where we want to be, we should keep two important points in mind. First, far more of our Father's children will be saved than we realize, and second, we need not live in doubt about our eternal status. The Lord has made it possible for us to know these things and to live our lives in the light or perspective they provide. President Harold B. Lee once observed: "Cyprian, the great defender of the Christian faith after the apostolic period, stated: 'Into my heart, purified of all sin, there entered a light which came from on high and then suddenly, and in a marvelous manner, I saw certainty succeed doubt'" (*Stand Ye in Holy Places*, 57).

In a day of skepticism, a time of spreading cynicism, if any people in all the wide world have a reason to be optimistic and forward-looking, it is the followers of Jesus the Christ. The gospel is the good news, the glad tidings that redemption from the fall and deliverance from death and hell are available to those who come unto Christ, accept his gospel, join his church, congregate with the faithful, and abide by the precepts set forth in scripture and in the teachings of prophets. There are absolute truths, constants in a world of shifting values. We may face a financial crisis, but forgiveness of sins is still available to those who repent. We may have a wandering child, but the power of the blood of Christ and the gift of the Holy Ghost are still available to soothe, strengthen, and sanctify the human heart. We may not get a job we had planned on, but the promise of the immortality of the soul and the eventual inseparable union of body and spirit will come to pass in God's own time. Hell may rage and the demons of destruction may taunt us in these last days, but there is a heaven prepared for those who love and serve the Lord Jesus Christ.

This book is about hope in Christ, about why we have reason to believe that we have a pretty good shot at happiness and joy here and the highest of eternal glories hereafter. Life is not easy, and challenges come to all of us at one time or another. Discouragement raises its ugly head, and Satan would have us lose perspective and thereby lose hope. But that need not happen. We have been given a solid doctrinal foundation for our hope, a spiritual and rational basis for believing in our grand possibilities. That this short work will assist us in discovering or reinforcing such hope is my sincere prayer.

ONE

What Are My Odds?

IT WOULD BE A TERRIBLE THING to commit ourselves to the Lord by covenant, accept him as our Lord and Savior, receive the ordinances of salvation, devote our lives to his work and glory, and then discover at the end of our gospel journey that we didn't make the cut, that our puny and paltry offering simply wasn't enough to qualify for the highest heaven. What a letdown that would be! Such a thought has caused me deep personal reflections over the years, long periods of introspection in which I found myself in prayer asking the One who knows best: "Am I on course? Is what I am doing the best use of my time? Is the path I'm pursuing the one Thou would have me pursue? If I continue in my present course, will I "get there"?

As a boy I wondered if I would ever live a good enough life to dwell hereafter in the same place as President David O. McKay. I wondered if I would ever have the strength and stamina and sticking power to remain faithful all my days, like President Larson, my stake president. I marveled at my grandfather Anatole Millet—his knowledge of the gospel and his powerful and persuasive manner of preaching—and I had great difficulty imagining a time when the scriptures and the words of the prophets would flow from my lips with such ease. As a teenager I wondered whether in my life I would be able to say "I know" with the same certitude as Sister Whitney or Brother Dixon. A full-time mission helped to establish a solid foundation for my life in terms of my testimony, and my later work in the Church Educational System gave me the privilege and opportunity to study and learn more and more about the restored gospel. Yet I still had difficulty fathoming that I would ever measure up to what had become through the years an almost impossible standard of purity and knowledge. I fell short, and I knew it.

My orientation and my outlook on life changed in the fall of 1976. One night my wife, Shauna, and I gathered with about five hundred other teachers from the Church Educational System for an evening with Elder Bruce R. McConkie. We met in a chapel at the institute of religion near the University of Utah in Salt Lake City. Because of his calling as a member of the Council of the Twelve Apostles, our admiration and respect for his gospel scholarship, and the meaningful occasions we had enjoyed with him before, we came to the meeting prepared to be filled. We were not disappointed. He spoke for about half an hour on the implications of the recent reorganization of the First Quorum of the Seventy. He spoke of priesthood, keys, and succession. Then he invited questions from the group. Some of the questions related to the seminary course of study for the year; others were about doctrinal matters in general. One question, and the answer that followed, changed my life; they affected the way I thereafter understood God, the plan of salvation, and how the gospel should be taught.

A young seminary teacher in the back of the chapel asked, in essence, "Elder McConkie, as you know, we are studying the New Testament in seminary this year. How do we keep our students from being discouraged (and how do we avoid discouragement ourselves) when we read in the scriptures that strait is the gate and narrow is the way that leads to life and few there be that find it?"

I will never forget Elder McConkie's powerful but totally unexpected answer. He stood up straight at the pulpit and said, "You tell your students that far more of our Father's children will be exalted than we think!" A stunned silence was followed by the expelling of air

7

(such as a person would experience when he has been hit in the stomach by a baseball bat), and then the chapel erupted in guarded but animated chatter among the teachers. The seminary teacher rose to his feet again and said, "I don't understand that. Could you please explain what you mean?"

"I'd be pleased to," Elder McConkie said.

What followed was one of the most enlightening and eye-opening discussions I have ever been involved with. Thinking back, I suppose it lasted for twenty or thirty minutes. After this many years, it is obviously impossible to recall the exact words that were spoken, but I remember as if it were yesterday many of the important ideas that Elder McConkie sought to convey, and, more particularly, what I felt. In substance and thought content and certainly in spirit, this is what was said: Indeed, the scriptures speak often of a strait and narrow path that leads to eternal life and frequently emphasize that few of the sons and daughters of God will find their way to the end of that path. But these are scriptural passages that must be viewed in proper perspective. In the long run, we must ever keep in mind that our Father and God is a successful Parent, one who will save far more of his children than he will lose. If that seems startling at first, we need to ponder for a moment.

In comparison to the number of wicked souls at any given time, the number of faithful followers may seem small. But what of the children who have died before the age of accountability—billions of little ones from the days of Adam to the time of the Second Coming, of whom the scriptures affirm that they are saved in the celestial kingdom of heaven? (D&C 137:10). What of those through the ages who never had the opportunity to hear the message of salvation in this life but who (because of the yearnings in their heart for light and truth) will receive it in the post-mortal spirit world?

And, we might ask, "What of the hosts of the righteous who qualified for salvation from Enoch's city, Melchizedek's Salem, the golden era of the Nephites, or other holy societies of which we have no record? (D&C 49:8). What of the countless billions of those children to be born during the glorious millennial era—a time when disease and death and sin as we know it have neither sting nor victory over humankind?" This will be that time of which the revelations speak, when "children shall grow up without sin unto salvation" (D&C 45:58).

Given the renewed and paradisiacal state of the earth, it may well be that more persons will live on the earth during the thousand years of our Lord's reign—

persons who are of at least a terrestrial nature—than the combined total of all who have lived during the previous six thousand years of the earth's temporal existence. Indeed, Elder McConkie asked us, "who can count the number of saved beings in eternity?" Our God, who is triumphant in all battles against the forces of evil, will surely be victorious in the numbers of his children who will be saved.

At that point, when we as a congregation were riding a spiritual high, Elder McConkie popped our balloon momentarily: "But all of that doesn't have much to do with you and me, does it?"

We sheepishly nodded in agreement and came back to earth. And then he explained that Latter-day Saints who chart their course toward eternal life, receive the ordinances of salvation, and strive with all their heart to be true to their covenants will gain eternal life. Even though they are certainly not perfect when they die, if they have sought to stay on course, in covenant, in harmony with the mind and will of God, they will be saved in the highest heaven.

We ought to have hope, he counseled us. We need to be positive and optimistic about making it. He startled us then with, "I would suppose, for example, that I am now looking out upon a group of men and women who will all go to the celestial kingdom."

We left the chapel both electrified and sobered. That night I lay awake pondering on what I had heard, and I reflected on it again and again in the days that followed. Shortly thereafter I sat down at the end of a very full and tiring Sabbath and turned on the television to watch a Brigham Young University devotional. To my surprise, the address was by Elder Bruce R. McConkie. It was a rebroadcast of a fireside he had delivered to the students entitled "Jesus Christ and Him Crucified." After discussing the plan of salvation, the greatest truths and heresies in all eternity, and the vital role of Jesus Christ as Redeemer, Elder McConkie said:

"As members of the Church, if we chart a course leading to eternal life; if we begin the processes of spiritual rebirth, and are going in the right direction; if we chart a course of sanctifying our souls, and degree by degree are going in that direction; and if we chart a course of becoming perfect, and, step by step and phase by phase, are perfecting our souls by overcoming the world, then it is absolutely guaranteed—there is no question whatever about it—we shall gain eternal life. Even though we have spiritual rebirth ahead of us, perfection ahead of us, the full degree of sanctification ahead of us, if we chart a course and follow it to the best of our ability in this life, then when we go out of this life we'll continue in exactly that same course" (*Speeches of the Year, 1976,* 400–401; see also Conference Report, October 1976, 158–59; "The Seven Deadly Heresies," *Speeches of the Year, 1980,* 78–79).

We must never forget that there is no ceiling on the number of saved beings in eternity, no cap, no quota by which the Father of us all must be governed. Like any parent, he surely desires that all of his sons and daughters receive the message of salvation, work righteousness, and return to him honorably. Not all will; that is true. But many will. A great many.

Father Lehi, as a part of his dream-vision, beheld men and women from all walks of life (1 Nephi 8). In what might well be called the parable of the paths, Lehi saw how four groups of people respond to truth and to what degree they are attracted to the good and the holy. This parable of the paths, like the parable of the soils in Matthew 13, is a study of spiritual receptivity.

Lehi saw one group that attained the strait and narrow path but wandered off the path and were lost because of the mists of darkness or temptations of the devil. A second group pressed forward to the end of the path and partook of the fruit. They were then lured away from further participation in gospel living because of embarrassment as a result of the taunting and ridicule from the worldly wise in the large and spacious building. A fourth group never made it to the path but instead blindly felt their way toward the large and spacious building.

Of those in the third group, however, Nephi said that his father "saw other multitudes pressing forward; and they came and caught hold of the end of the rod of iron; and they did press their way forward, continually holding fast to the rod of iron, until they came forth and fell down and partook of the fruit of the tree" (1 Nephi 8:30). And what became of them? We suppose they stayed faithful and endured to the end. They were saved. And how many were there? *Multitudes.*

In a similar vein, President Joseph F. Smith, who was blessed to behold in vision the postmortal spirit world only six weeks before his own entrance into it, remarked: "As I pondered over these things which are written"—the writings of the third and fourth chapters of the First Epistle of Peter—"the eyes of my understanding were opened, and the Spirit of the Lord rested upon me, and I saw the hosts of the dead, both small and great. And there were gathered together in one place"—we know it as paradise—"*an innumerable company of the spirits of the just, who had been faithful in the testimony of Jesus while they lived in mortality. . . .* All these had departed the mortal life, firm in the hope of a glorious resurrection, through the grace of God the

Father and his Only Begotten Son, Jesus Christ" (D&C 138:11–14; emphasis added).

It has been my privilege to associate with good men and women most of my life, men and women of faith and character, men and women who have received the gospel of Jesus Christ and are striving to abide by its precepts. They are people who are earnestly seeking to serve the sheep of his fold and make a difference for good in a world that is in desperate need of goodness. They are people of covenant, people who have come out of the world and yearn to put off the natural man and come unto Christ. But they are not perfect. They make mistakes, feel regret, and often wonder about their standing before God.

Satan works tirelessly to lead us into major transgression. He also strives to discourage us whenever we fall short of the standards we and God have set for ourselves. We simply must not let him discourage us. I have a witness, burned into my soul as if by fire, that God is mindful of his children and that he has established a divine plan for the ultimate transformation of man and society. I also know that we can make it, make it to the celestial kingdom, if we stay on the gospel path, trust in and rely upon him who is mighty to save, press on, and never, never give up.

This understanding is not based upon the power of

positive thinking, although we surely should be positive. It is not an effort to bury our heads in the sand and ignore the widening waves of wickedness or to minimize the fact that none of us is perfect. Rather, this understanding is based on sound doctrinal teachings in harmony with what the prophets have taught through the ages. They bring peace to my soul and color all that I do and say as a gospel teacher, a husband, a father, and a grandfather. While we must never be arrogant or self-assured in any way when it comes to the matter of our salvation, we need not yield to false modesty, false doctrine (the notion that few, if any, will make it), or false feelings of inadequacy. There is a better way to live our lives, a more excellent way, one that comes through him who *is* the Way.

TWO

What's Good Enough?

MOST OF US SUPPOSE THAT we need to be "good" to qualify for eternal life. What does that mean? You will recall that a lawyer approached Jesus and asked the rather straightforward question: "Good Master, what good thing shall I do, that I may have eternal life?" Rather than getting right to the point, of setting forth specific requirements for the highest heaven, the Savior answered, "Why callest thou me good? *There is none good but one, that is, God*" (Matthew 19:16–17; emphasis added).

What an odd answer! Wasn't Jesus good? Was he not sinless? Had he not kept the ordinances and laws of the Father with exactness? In fact, did he not live what we have come to know as a "perfect life"? I have pondered upon this passage for many years now, and a couple of thoughts have come to mind. Could it be that Jesus was essentially inquiring of the lawyer, "So you call me good, do you? Since God is the only truly good man, are you acknowledging me as God? Do you accept my divine Sonship? Do you receive my claim to divinity?"

Another possibility is that Jesus Christ simply did here what he did regularly and consistently—he deferred to the Father in all things. He came to earth to carry out not his own will but rather the Father's. His doctrine was not his but rather the doctrine of the One who had sent him, namely, the Father. He did nothing but what he had seen the Father do. In short, Jesus constantly deflected fame and honor and glory to where it should always be, to the ultimate source of his worship and ours—our Heavenly Father.

So let's get practical for a minute. Was Jesus good? Of course he was. He embodied goodness. Was Jesus pure and holy and free from taint of any kind? Without question he was. Like the Father, he is the Standard, the Guide, or what the Prophet Joseph Smith called the prototype of all saved beings (*Lectures on Faith,* 7:9). "Who, among all the Saints in these last days," the Prophet asked, "can consider himself as good as our Lord? Who is as perfect? Who is as pure? Who is as holy as He was? Are they to be found? He never transgressed or broke a commandment or law of heaven—no deceit was in His mouth, neither was guile found in His heart" (*Teachings of the Prophet Joseph Smith,* 67). On a later occasion, Brother Joseph observed: "I do not think there have been many good men on the earth since the days of Adam; but *there was one good man and his name was Jesus*" (*Teachings of the Prophet Joseph Smith,* 303; emphasis added; see also 187–88, 266).

While the standard of what is good and what is bad is solid and firm and fixed, He who is the Standard is patient and loving and long-suffering. Our God is more than an unyielding force; he is our Father in Heaven, and he has tender regard for all of his children. Similarly, our Divine Redeemer is more than a "catch me if you can" leader who runs ahead of his troops; he is the Good Shepherd, who goes in search of his lost sheep, one who calls to his little ones, "Come, follow me." His patient pleadings and tender tutorials reflect the comforting fact that he is "touched with the feeling of our infirmities" (Hebrews 4:15). As Max Lucado pointed out, "God loves you just the way you are, but he refuses to leave you that way. He wants you to be just like Jesus" (*Just like Jesus,* 3). In other words, he loves us, and he will, through the power of his blood, make us good. As one person has wisely observed, there will be no good people in heaven, *only forgiven ones* (Stanley, *How Good Is Good Enough?* 63).

Understanding this concept should lead to hope, "a more excellent hope" than anything the world has to offer (Ether 12:32). It was the apostle Paul who called upon the Christian soldier to "put on the whole armour of God, that ye may be able to stand against the wiles of the devil. For we wrestle not against flesh and blood, but against principalities, against powers, against the rulers of the darkness of this world, against spiritual wickedness in high places. Wherefore take unto you the whole armour of God, that ye may be able to withstand in the evil day, and having done all, to stand" (Ephesians 6:11–13). A different translation of verse 12 makes interesting reading: "For our struggle is not against human foes, but against cosmic powers, against the authorities and potentates of this dark age, against the superhuman forces of evil in the heavenly realms" (Revised English Bible).

Paul named several pieces of armor and battle tactics: girding our loins with truth; having on the breastplate of righteousness; putting on the shoes of the preparation of the gospel of peace; wielding the shield of faith; taking the helmet of salvation; and employing the power of the sword of the Holy Spirit (Ephesians 6:11–17). In writing to the Thessalonian Saints, Paul encouraged the members of the household of faith to stand as "children of light" in being ready and prepared to receive the Lord Jesus when he returns in glory: "But let us, who are of the day, be sober, putting on the breastplate of faith and love; and for an helmet, *the hope of salvation*" (1 Thessalonians 5:5, 8; emphasis added).

Think about it. It's not just salvation that becomes our helmet in the war against Satan and his hosts but the helmet of the *hope of salvation*. Saving faith in Christ gives birth to hope in Christ (Moroni 7:40–42)—anticipation, expectation, and assurance—that we will inherit salvation through the unearned divine assistance, unmerited divine favor, enabling power, the grace of our Lord and Savior. Such a hope, borne of the Spirit, results in a quiet but dynamic confidence, a sweet, settled, and compelling expectation that replaces doubt and fear.

THREE

From Weakness to Strength

As I HAVE WORKED IN THE Church over the years as a bishop, a stake president, and a religious educator, I have encountered many capable, competent, and impressive Latter-day Saints. Like all of us, they wrestle with challenges and struggle to be all they could be. In too many instances, however, I have spoken with my brothers and sisters of the need to learn to trust more in the Lord and less in the arm of flesh, only to have them (politely) reject my counsel and choose to face their issues alone. I suppose the most common response I have encountered is "It's okay. I can handle it." I think a close translation of "I can handle it" is "I can get by on my own. I don't want to trouble you or the Lord. God expects me to give it my best shot. I'm strong. I can deal with my own problems."

Although self-reliance is certainly a virtue worth incorporating in our lives, when carried to an extreme it becomes a vice, a deterrent, a roadblock to spiritual progress. For example, Alma's youngest son, Corianton, left the ministry and became involved in an immoral relationship with the harlot Isabel. Alma counseled him: "For thou didst not give so much heed unto my words as did thy brother [Shiblon], among the people of the Zoramites. Now this is what I have against thee; *thou didst go on unto boasting in thy strength and thy wisdom*" (Alma 39:2; emphasis added).

My guess is that Corianton did not walk down the streets with a button on his lapel or a sign in his hand that read, "I'm wonderful. I'm marvelous. I'm terrific. I'm the best there is." Rather, Corianton's boasting in his own strength and in his own wisdom probably entailed his unfounded and unwise trust in his own ability to handle things—in this case, to resist moral temptation. More specifically, he must have determined that he could fly close to the flame of sin and associate with the wrong people, including a prostitute, without getting burned. Corianton essentially said, "It's okay. I can handle it." And oh, how tragically wrong he was. Corianton suffered from pride and overmuch self-assurance, and it proved for a painful season to be his undoing. Oddly enough, many of those who yell the loudest that they can handle it are not handling things very well at all.

Both Paul and Moroni learned and then taught the time-honored lesson that it is through the humble acknowledgment of our weakness that we open ourselves to the divine enabling power of the Savior (2 Corinthians 12:9–10; Ether 12:27). It is when we are up against the wall of faith, stripped of personal confidence, and naked in our ineptitude that we recognize that we *can't* handle it. That simple admission, that moment of truth, that powerful confession has the effect of transferring not only our trust and our allegiance to the Omnipotent One but also shifting our confidence and reliance—and the fretting and worrying that accompany excessive self-reliance—to One who assumes the burden for us, the only One who is entitled to our complete trust. (We call that faith.)

"At first it is natural for a baby to take its mother's milk without knowing its mother," C. S. Lewis taught. "It is equally natural for us to see the man who helps us without seeing Christ behind him. But we must not remain babies. We must go on to recognize the real Giver. It is madness not to. Because, if we do not, we shall be relying on human beings. And that is going to let us down. The best of them will make mistakes; all of them will die. We must be thankful to all the people who have helped us, we must honour them and love them. But *never, never pin your whole faith on any human being:* not if he is the best and wisest in the whole world. There are lots of nice things you can do with sand; but do not try building a house on it" (*Mere Christianity,* 165; emphasis added).

Only a few months after being called to the Quorum of the Twelve Apostles, Elder Jeffrey R. Holland called me one Friday afternoon. "I'd like to come and see you, as well as visit with your faculty." (I was serving at the time as dean of Religious Education at Brigham Young University.)

I responded, "Great! When can you come?"

He replied, "How about Monday?"

I assured him that we would have a full house, and we would be honored to have him visit us for as long as he could stay.

On Monday Elder Holland and I chatted in my office for a little less than an hour before we entered the conference room, where a packed house of full-time religious educators waited. After a hymn and opening prayer, he spoke to the faculty for about ninety minutes. He delivered a powerful commission to be united and to see to it that what we taught was true and accompanied by the Spirit of God. He then invited questions. Someone asked him to share with us whatever he felt would be appropriate about his recent call to the Twelve. Elder Holland began by describing how shocked and ill-prepared he had felt when he had been called to the Seventy some five years earlier and yet how much more absolutely overwhelming his call to the Twelve had been. He mentioned how he had walked the floors at night, searching his soul introspectively, striving earnestly for the purification of his heart, an inner cleansing that he realized would be required of one called to serve as a special witness of the name of Christ in all the world. I remember well his poignant and emotional expression to us that he had lost all confidence in himself, in his ability to teach or to preach or "to lead a Primary class out of a brown paper bag." He said many more things that lifted and inspired us and gave us a deeper sense of the consecration associated with a call to the holy apostleship.

For weeks thereafter I pondered Elder Holland's words, particularly his comments about his loss of confidence, his unyielding sense of complete inadequacy. I wondered why. Why would a merciful and loving Lord exact such a price from one of his chosen witnesses? It began to dawn on me that this newest member of the Twelve was being shown painfully and persuasively just how much he would need to lean upon, rely upon, totally trust in, and exercise complete confidence in the Lord Jesus Christ. (We call that faith.) His strength would be the Master. His words would be the Master's. His very being would be forevermore consumed with knowing and carrying out the will of the Master.

The gospel of Jesus Christ is the grand news, the glad tidings that through our exercise of faith in Jesus Christ and his atonement, coupled with our repentance that flows therefrom, we may be forgiven of our sins and justified or made right with God. Our standing before the Almighty has thereby changed from a position of divine wrath to one of heavenly favor and acceptance; we have traveled the path from death to life (Romans 5:9–10). "Therefore being justified by faith, we have peace with God through our Lord Jesus Christ" (Romans 5:1). Or, as Peter taught, "Humble yourselves therefore under the mighty hand of God, that he may exalt you in due time: *casting all your care upon him; for he careth for you*" (1 Peter 5:6–7; emphasis added).

Surely it is the case that we can cast our burdens upon the Lord because he cares for us—that is, because he loves us. But more is intended by Peter in this passage. We can give away to him who is the Balm of Gilead our worries, our anxieties, our frettings, our awful anticipations, for he will care for us, that is, *he will do the caring for us.* It is as though Peter counsels us: "Quit worrying. Don't be so anxious. Stop wringing

26

your hands. Let Jesus take the burden while you take the peace."

To say that another way, grace represents God's acceptance of me. Faith represents my acceptance of God's acceptance of me. And peace is my acceptance of me. That is what C. S. Lewis meant when he pointed out that a maturing Christian despairs of doing anything on his own and "leaves it to God." In other words, a Christian leaves it to God when he "puts all his trust in Christ," thereby allowing the Savior to make up for the disciple's deficiencies. But this is a joint effort, God and man working together to save the human soul. And so while we learn to leave the burdens of life at the altar of Christ, we continue to do our very best to keep the commandments. "Thus if you have really handed yourself over to Him, it must follow that you are trying to obey Him. But *trying in a new way, a less worried way*" (Lewis, *Mere Christianity*, 130–31; emphasis added).

Let's be wise and honest: We cannot handle it. We cannot make it on our own. We cannot pull ourselves up by our own spiritual bootstraps. We are not bright enough or powerful enough to bring to pass the mighty change necessary to see and enter the kingdom of God. We cannot pry our way through the gates of the heavenly Jerusalem any more than we can perform our own eye surgery. We cannot make ourselves happy or bring about our own fulfillment. But we can "seek this Jesus of whom the prophets and apostles have written, that the grace of God the Father, and also the Lord Jesus Christ, and the Holy Ghost, which beareth record of them, may be and abide in [us] forever" (Ether 12:41). Then all these things will be added unto us (Matthew 6:33).

That's the promise, and I affirm that it's true.

FOUR

The Worth of Souls

PEOPLE MATTER. THEY MATTER a great deal. In fact, people matter more than anything. God and Christ are in the business of people (Moses 1:39), and so should we be. A dear friend of mine worked for a season in the Church Office Building. He was quite young, and yet he had been given significant responsibilities for a central program of the Church. He is a natural leader, and he became extremely efficient in his work, so efficient that over time product began to be valued more than persons. In other words, he got the job done quickly and well, but unfortunately he did so at the expense of people's feelings.

My friend shared with me that one of the general authorities drew him aside to compliment him on his efficiency and productivity. Then he added, "I have a simple recommendation, in the form of a principle, that I would like to share with you, if you're open to it."

"Of course," my friend replied, "I'm wide open for counsel."

The leader said, "Always remember that *people* are more important than truth."

My friend said that he recoiled and responded, "No, Elder——, nothing is more important than truth."

The general authority patiently repeated himself: "I assure you that from the Lord's perspective, people *are* more important than truth."

It was a lesson for a lifetime, one that at first pricked my friend's conscience but gradually changed his life and of course his administrative style.

Don't misunderstand. Of course truth is important. It is vital. We strive all the days of our lives to learn the truth, live the truth, and eventually qualify to be with him who is the Truth (John 14:6). We teach truth and seek always to present the message of salvation accurately, honestly, and truthfully. As Elder Russell M. Nelson has taught, however, truth cannot stand alone; we need to be certain that we present "truth *and more*" (*Power within Us,* 99–100).

Christian writer John Stackhouse has written: "God cares about people more than he cares about 'truth' in the abstract. *Jesus didn't die on the cross to make a point. He died on the cross to save people whom he loves.* We, too, must represent our Lord with love to God and our neighbor always foremost in our concerns" (*Humble Apologetics,* 142; emphasis added).

Again, people matter. People's feelings matter. That man or woman is most Christlike who focuses on how to bless individuals and families, how to lift and lighten the burdens of the burdened, how to attend to the troubles of the troubled. Policies and procedures and programs, although important in their own right, only exist to assist in loving and blessing the lives of others.

I have on several occasions held the hand of individuals who were dying, sanctified souls whose lives had equipped them to avoid the sting of death and seemed almost to rob the grim reaper of his victory. I have sensed deeply on those occasions the profound effect of one life on the whole of existence. I have often expressed to God in prayer my sincere gratitude for my teachers, my advisers, my priesthood leaders, my mission presidents and their wives, and caring souls in general who for some reason chose to take the time to take an interest in me and in my welfare. The ripple effect of one good person is absolutely immeasurable.

In June 1829 Oliver Cowdery and David Whitmer

were taught that "the worth of souls is great" (D&C 18:10). Why is this the case?

We may answer that the worth of souls is great because we were created by a God, and he does not create unnecessary things. We could add that we are the children of God and thus inherit his likeness and image. We could point out that as children of God we have unlimited possibilities, infinite potential to accomplish a world of good. As Christian writer John Stott noted, "When human beings are valued as persons, because of their intrinsic worth, everything changes. Why? Because people matter. Because every man, woman, and child has worth and significance as a human being made in God's image and likeness" (*Why I Am a Christian,* 106–7).

All of these answers are correct. But another answer lies beneath and stretches beyond these ideas.

Brothers Cowdery and Whitmer were taught that "the worth of souls is great" because "the Lord your Redeemer suffered death in the flesh; wherefore he suffered the pain of all men, that all men might repent and come unto him. And he hath risen again from the dead, that he might bring all men unto him, on conditions of repentance. And how great is his joy in the soul that repenteth!" (D&C 18:11–13).

The apostle Peter observed that as followers of the

Savior we are "a peculiar people" (1 Peter 2:9). We are peculiar in that we do not take our cues from the world; we march to a very different drummer. We do not establish our values based on social consensus; we know what is right and what is wrong because of the light of Christ, the gift of the Holy Ghost, and the teachings of scripture and prophetic oracles. The world and the worldly may be marching to Babylon by the most direct route, but we are marching to Zion, to righteousness, to glory. The world may be jettisoning time-honored truths and dismantling the family, but we are standing up, standing out, and thus holding out for a society of the pure in heart in which the family unit may be perpetuated everlastingly. And so, from the world's point of view, the Latter-day Saints—and all people who are prepared to engage worldliness and relativism—are peculiar in that we are different from the world.

More important, however, we are peculiar in that we are a *purchased* people. "What? Know ye not that your body is the temple of the Holy Ghost which is in you, which ye have of God, and *ye are not your own. For ye are bought with a price:* therefore glorify God in your body, and in your spirit, which are God's" (1 Corinthians 6:19–20; emphasis added; compare 7:23; 1 Peter 1:18–19).

In short, the worth of souls is great in the sight of God because an infinite price has been paid for our souls, a dear price that represents God's greatest gift to us—namely, the redemption wrought through the atonement of his Only Begotten Son, Jesus Christ.

No one of us is without flaw. We all make mistakes. We all fall short. We all feel the pangs of conscience. It's not all bad that we are occasionally plagued by our consciences. It has been my lot to work with people who are past feeling, who no longer experience guilt or remorse, even over heinous deeds. I have worked with persons who can no longer discern what is true from what is false; having lied and deceived others so many, many times in the past, they are no longer capable of choosing the right.

After working with such persons I find myself praying often, "Oh, Heavenly Father, please strengthen my conscience; help me to feel what I ought to feel." Our conscience serves in the spiritual realm the same function that pain serves in the physical body. If we could not feel pain when we were near a fire or when our feet were freezing, we would be in a most serious condition.

To the extent that we strive to do our best and keep the commandments, the light of Christ will clarify our vision of what is right and what is wrong, heighten our

34

sensitivity to good and evil, and make known the will of the Almighty in a clear and unmistakable manner (Moroni 7:15–16). Elder Bruce C. Hafen declared, "If you have problems in your life, don't assume there is something wrong with you. Struggling with those problems is at the very core of life's purpose. As we draw close to God, He will show us our weaknesses and through them make us wiser, stronger. If you're seeing more of your weaknesses, that just might mean you're moving nearer to God, not farther away" (Conference Report, April 2004, 100).

Indeed, some of the purest men and women who have lived on this earth have readily acknowledged their weakness before God—their mortality, their limitations, their inability to win the victory alone. When such stalwart defenders of the faith as Paul and Nephi cry out, "O wretched man that I am" (Romans 7:24; 2 Nephi 4:17), some of us in the rank and file of humankind may remark that we would die to be as wretched as Nephi! Or we might be tempted to throw in the towel and ask in introspective pain: "If *they* are wretched, then what possible chance do I have?"

My testimony is that we have a very good chance, an excellent chance, if we can learn to see things in proper perspective and live our lives in the light of that perspective. We need to learn to achieve that delicate balance between divine discontent (or sanctified dissatisfaction) and what Nephi called a "perfect brightness of hope" (2 Nephi 31:20). We who have come out of the world unto Christ by covenant have placed ourselves on a path that leads ultimately to eternal life. We need to stay on the path, keep walking, and bounce up whenever we fall. The Keeper of the Gate, the Holy One of Israel, has not placed a ceiling on the number of saved beings; rather, he is ready and willing to heal and empower and redeem and save all who desire these consummate blessings. He is with us at the starting gate of life's race, travels along the pathway with us, and waits at the finish line, not alone to certify us but, more important, to welcome us home.

While the power is within us to choose good over evil (2 Nephi 2:16; D&C 58:28), to discern and eschew those beggarly elements of the world that degrade, we need the Lord God desperately to become worthy and to stay that way. We not only need his forgiveness from sin but also his enabling power to carry out those duties and undergo that change that will make us one day just as he is. "As for me," the Psalmist affirmed, "I will behold thy face in righteousness: I shall be satisfied, when I awake, with thy likeness" (Psalm 17:15). Or, as John proclaimed, "when he shall appear, we shall be like him"—fully worthy—"for we shall see him as he is" (1 John 3:2). For that day I long. To that end I trust in and rely upon Him who says to you and me now, in essence, "You're not there yet, but you're pointed in the right direction. Stay with it."

FIVE

Does God Grade on the Curve?

ONE OF THE FIRST COURSES I enrolled in as a psychology major was Psychological Statistics. I had been warned that Stats was a tough course, so I decided to take it early and get it over with. The young assistant professor walked into the room the first day of class and said: "Let's begin by pointing out that there are fourteen of you in the class. You need an A in this course to be accepted into graduate school. And you need to know that only three of you will receive an A."

It's hard to describe the mixture of feelings that washed over me (and, I presume, the other students) at that precise moment. Fear. Anxiety. Frustration. Suspicion. As you might expect, those remarks created a competitive spirit and mood of isolation that few other things could have brought about. I learned a great deal that semester, but I didn't make many friends; it was literally everyone for himself.

As fate would have it, when I completed my master's degree in psychology, the department chair asked me to teach a couple of classes as a graduate instructor. Yes, they were Psychological Statistics. I marched into class the first day, welcomed the students, and said, "Let's begin by pointing out that there are fourteen of you in the class. You need an A in this course to be accepted into graduate school. And you need to know that as far as I'm concerned you all have an A, starting right now, unless you prove me wrong. So let's work together, focus on what needs to be done, and everyone should be just fine."

The mood that semester was completely different: There was a spirit of friendliness and openness and sharing that made for an enjoyable learning experience. No one felt compared to anyone else, and all felt the need to do their best and lift one another in the process.

I've been associated with higher education long enough now to know that competition is "where it's at," especially in such programs as pre-med and pre-law. And I've brushed up against the world of business and industry enough to acknowledge that comparison and competition between employees are used quite often to bolster productivity. But what place do they have in the gospel of Jesus Christ? Is there any benefit to be derived from comparing ourselves with others on how long we prayed last night or how many pages of scripture we read or how many hours we fasted or how long it has been since we uttered a profanity? Is it God's practice to say to Sister Bancroft, "Now, Mildred, I surely wish you would bear your testimony a little more like Sister Allen. She's great!"? Or to Brother Harrison, "Fred, you might want to pay attention to how Brother Atkinson cares for his home teaching families. I really wish you were more like him"?

It sounds rather ludicrous, doesn't it? Our Heavenly Father simply doesn't work that way. Such comments are neither motivating nor in any way uplifting.

Then why do we choose to compare ourselves with others? Why do we set up standards of spirituality that are really quite shallow and superficial? In this get-ahead world, this driven and highly competitive climate in which we live and move and have our being, it's a wonder that anyone discerns the relevant from the irrelevant. It's easy to forget what President Joseph F. Smith taught: "To do well those things which God ordained to be the common lot of all man-kind, is the truest greatness" (*Gospel Doctrine*, 285).

I was sitting in a Sunday School class once when the teacher began to address this very issue— comparing ourselves to one another. He warned of the hazards of doing so and added: "We should never compare ourselves or our situations in life to others. If you must compare yourself to someone, then compare yourself to Christ, for he is our Exemplar." I reflected on that comment for quite a while that day and found myself thinking, "Compare ourselves with Christ. Well, that certainly makes me feel better! From now on I will lay my deeds and my puny offerings next to his, and then I can really get (and stay) depressed."

The truth is, comparing just doesn't work. Period. We will either maintain a constant feeling of inadequacy or cultivate an inappropriate view of our own importance. Neither is healthy. Even some of Jesus' disciples were tempted to seek for positions of prominence, and the Master chastened them with the words, "Whosoever will be great among you, let him be your minister; and whosoever will be chief among you, let him be your servant" (Matthew 20:26–27; compare Mark 10:28–41). Jesus himself set the standard and abolished all forms of spiritual pecking orders when he, the greatest man to traverse earth's paths, described his role as "I am among you as he that serveth" (Luke 22:27).

One writer put this all into perspective when he asked: "When you die, do you get to go to heaven if your good deeds constitute 70 percent of your overall deeds? Or does 51 percent earn you a passing grade?

. . . Or what if God's holiness and perfection outweigh his mercy and he requires that 90 percent of our deeds be good? Or what if God grades on a curve and Mother Teresa skewed the cosmic curve, raising the bar for good deeds beyond what most of us are capable of?" (Stanley, *How Good Is Good Enough?* 45–46).

While for Latter-day Saints salvation is a family affair, coming unto Christ by covenant and carrying out the will of God is an individual undertaking. When it comes to standing at the bar of judgment, a summary of our lives (including our good deeds) will not be placed alongside anyone else's. We are baptized one by one, confirmed one by one, ordained one by one, set apart one by one, and endowed one by one. And even though we kneel in the house of the Lord opposite the love of our life in the highest ordinance this side of heaven, the keeping of temple covenants and ultimately the matter of being conformed to the image of Christ Jesus is accomplished one soul at a time. We are all in this together. Not one of us is exempt from the examinations of mortality or receives a bye in the game of life. We're here to do the best we can. The quest for spirituality doesn't entail our being morphed into the image of another human but rather to have God, through his Holy Spirit, make us into all that he desires us to be.

SIX

" . . . Forgiven; For She Loved Much"

WHETHER WE ARE "THERE YET" has little to do with how one life compares with another's. There are so many unknowns, so many factors that are unseen or unsuspected in each of our lives—be they health challenges, family struggles, or perpetuated false traditions—for any of us to suppose that we know all about Brother Johnson or Sister Trujillo and wish we could be like them.

All the Lord asks is our best shot. I don't need to be unnaturally pious to be acceptable, nor need I to be truer than true. Elder James E. Talmage encouraged the Latter-day Saints to "be mindful of the fact that whether it be the gift of a man or a nation, the best, if offered willingly and with pure intent, is always excellent in the sight of God, however poor by other comparison that best may be" (*House of the Lord,* 3). Similarly, President Gordon B. Hinckley counseled the people of the covenant to "do the best that you can. The Lord doesn't expect you to do more than that" (*Church News,* 31 August 2002, 3).

Consider the account of the widow's mite. "And Jesus sat over against the treasury, and beheld how the people cast money into the treasury: and many that were rich cast in much. And there came a certain poor widow, and she threw in two mites, which make a farthing. And he called unto him his disciples, and saith unto them, Verily I say unto you, That this poor widow hath cast more in, than all they which have cast into the treasury: for all they did cast in of their abundance; but she of her want did cast in all that she had, even all her living" (Mark 12:41–44).

This poor widow gave the least that she could give (no less than two mites was acceptable), but, we would suppose, she gave the maximum she could afford. Jesus' commendation of her actions suggests that she gave all she had, which, from an eternal perspective, is worth more than the massive surplus of the affluent, at least of the affluent who give in order to be seen of men. When it costs us little to give, the eternal reward is a small one. Jesus said on another occasion that "out of the abundance of the heart the mouth speaketh" (Matthew 12:34). To be sure, our actions, not just our conversation, reveal our heart. In this case, the poor widow gave abundantly because her motives were pure and her consecration was complete. And her offering speaks volumes, for truly "God loveth a cheerful giver" (2 Corinthians 9:7).

This story holds a place in the hearts of millions. Perhaps that is because each of us feels our offering to God or to humankind to be so inadequate, so painfully paltry, that we identify with the poor widow. The message of the story is invigorating: God judges by a different standard. His thoughts are not our thoughts, neither are his ways our ways (Isaiah 55:8–9). Truly, "the Lord seeth not as man seeth; for man looketh on the outward appearance, but the Lord looketh on the heart" (1 Samuel 16:7). Far too often we are prone to judge others' success by their income, the kind of automobile they drive, or the clothing they wear. Far too often we judge a person's contribution by its monetary value. But the Omniscient One sees things differently. When a person gives all he has, that is all that is expected.

The story of the widow's mite is a story about consecration, about surrendering all that we have and are to a cause greater and grander than anything the world has to offer. When we consecrate ourselves to God, for example, we "make sacred" the offering of time, talents, and means to the building of God's kingdom. We give all that we have to God. All of it. But to be fully consecrated requires more than our wallet: It requires our will. To be sure, it is not easy to part with niceties that we have worked hard to acquire. But it is even more challenging to surrender desires, hopes, and dreams to the higher cause.

In the long run, as Elder Neal A. Maxwell pointed out, "the submission of one's will is really the only uniquely personal thing we have to place on God's altar. The many other things we 'give,' brothers and sisters, are actually the things He has already given or loaned to us. However, when you and I finally submit ourselves, by letting our individual wills be swallowed up in God's will, then we are really giving something to Him! It is the only possession which is truly ours to give! Consecration thus constitutes the only unconditional surrender which is also a total victory!" (Conference Report, October 1995, 30).

Further, "our perfect Father," Elder Maxwell observed, "does not expect us to be perfect children yet. He had only one such Child. Meanwhile, therefore, sometimes with smudges on our cheeks, dirt on our hands, and shoes untied, stammeringly but smilingly we present God with a dandelion—as if it were an orchid or a rose! If for now the dandelion is the best we have to offer, He receives it, knowing what we may later place on the altar. It is good to remember how young we are spiritually" (*Maxwell Quote Book,* 243).

Freedom of soul comes to us when we learn to unshackle ourselves from this world's toys, when we are no longer possessed by our possessions. Freedom of soul comes to us when we are willing to give to God that which, from an eternal perspective, is not much but is all we have. Like the poor widow, once we have placed our all in the divine treasury, we walk away with a lighter purse but a lighter soul. Such sacred surrender results in release, in peace, in quiet joy. It describes the abundant life.

When I was a young man, I was the junior companion in a ward teaching assignment to a couple who had been in the Church for a short time. I'll call them Becky and Gary Stewart. They were recent converts to the Church. They had a strong testimony of the gospel, loved the Lord (both had been brought up in Christian homes), and wanted to do all they could to show their gratitude to God for the newfound blessing that had come into their life. They were always at church, active and involved in all its programs, and deeply devoted to their beautiful little family. They wanted so much to go to the temple to make theirs an eternal marriage and to have their children sealed to them. There was only one problem: Becky wrestled with a smoking habit.

She had stopped smoking during the weeks the missionaries taught them, and for some time it appeared that the "rotten habit" (as she called it) was gone. But during a family crisis and following some extraordinarily stressful situations, her resistance waned, and she began to smoke again. She tried hard to stop. She did everything she knew how, but the craving persisted. She would stop for a few weeks or months and then slip back into the habit again. Discouragement, depression, disappointment, and a lake of tears would follow. We wept and prayed and labored with her for years.

Gary was an unusual man. He was a great provider, a loving father, and a person possessed of almost infinite patience and understanding for his wife. He obviously wanted to receive the blessings of the house of the Lord as much as Becky did, but he never allowed his eagerness to be sealed as a family to squelch one ounce of loving kindness toward Becky. Becky, too, was remarkable. She never yielded to the temptation to stay home from church until she had solved her problem; somehow she realized that everyone wrestles with something, be it a temper, gossip, financial stresses, marital discord, or whatever. And so to her eternal credit, Becky was always there, always right in the middle of church activities, especially service projects. Feeling less worthy than her brothers and sisters around her, she always volunteered for scrubbing the floors, cleaning the chapel, or carrying out other assignments that few would jump to get.

It took a number of years, a ton of prayers and blessings, and a tenacity that few of us can comprehend, but eventually the Stewarts went to the temple. I know Becky well enough to know that even now, once in a very great while, she will slip up and have a cigarette. She will go through the ordeal of remorse, regret, repentance, and recommitment, and jump back into the fray. The "rotten habit" isn't gone from her completely, but she's much better now than she was thirty years ago. And her waters run much deeper. Her struggles to resist, her pleadings for strength, her dream of being free from this enslaving habit, and her untiring devotion to the Lord's kingdom—these things have had a sanctifying effect upon her soul, even though she still wrestles with her addiction. She is possessed of a depth of love, tenderness, and compassion that most of us would love to acquire one day before we die. I know from personal experience that our Heavenly Father loves Becky Stewart. And Becky Stewart loves him.

My experience in knowing the Stewarts is reminiscent of an incident in the New Testament. "And one of the Pharisees desired [Jesus] that he would eat with him. And he went into the Pharisee's house, and sat down to meat. And, behold, a woman in the city, which was a sinner, when she knew that Jesus sat at meat in the Pharisee's house, brought an alabaster box of ointment, and stood at his feet behind him weeping, and began to wash his feet with tears, and did wipe them with the hairs of her head, and kissed his feet, and anointed them with the ointment" (Luke 7:36–38).

When the host, Simon the Pharisee, saw this, he was disgusted. He seems to have thought, "If this man is really the Messiah, the Son of God, as he claims to be, how could he not be repulsed by this sinful woman's actions? Why would a holy man allow one so very unholy to anoint his feet?"

Jesus perceived Simon's self-righteousness and scolded him by suggesting that this woman was much more thoughtful and cordial than the host himself had been: Simon had not rushed forward to wash and anoint the Savior's dusty feet, an appropriate social gesture in Israel. Then the Master went on to teach an invaluable and timeless lesson: "Wherefore I say unto thee, *Her sins, which are many, are forgiven; for she loved much:* but to whom little is forgiven, the same loveth little. And [Jesus] said unto her, Thy sins are forgiven. . . . Thy faith hath saved thee; go in peace" (Luke 7:47–50; emphasis added).

I am both haunted and stirred by the Lord's words:

"Her sins, which are many, are forgiven; for she loved much." What does this mean? What was the Savior trying to teach her, to teach Simon, to teach the people at the banquet, to teach you and me? Is this message related in some way to the injunction of James, the brother of the Lord? "Brethren, if any of you do err from the truth," James wrote, "and one convert him; let him know, that he which converteth the sinner from the error of his way shall save a soul from death, and shall hide a multitude of sins" (James 5:19–20). It sounds like two souls are being saved here, the wanderer and the helper. Is it related somehow to what Peter taught? "And above all things have fervent charity among yourselves: for *charity shall cover the multitude of sins*" (1 Peter 4:8; emphasis added; JST: "charity *preventeth* a multitude of sins"; emphasis added).

Some things simply matter more to our all-loving Lord than they matter to mortal men and women. Bowing humbly and reverentially before the Redeemer, confessing our weakness, rendering service, making sacrifices, being willing to be inconvenienced, lifting and strengthening one who has fallen, expressing loving kindness—these are the tokens of true Christianity, the emblems of discipleship, the coin of the celestial realm. They manifest to God and to ourselves who and what we have become.

SEVEN

An Attitude of Gratitude

A FRIEND OF MINE, A MEMBER of another faith, has become a treasured acquaintance. He is a superb scholar, a historian and theologian who is respected and admired by many within the academy. His articles are penetrating, and his books are thorough and groundbreaking. He is bright and capable and articulate, to be sure. He thinks and talks about profound things; his waters run deep. More important, however, Jim is a gracious and caring soul who seems to live in and exude a spirit of gratitude and thanksgiving. He is a happy man, one who loves his wife and children, cherishes time with his grandchildren, and always, always rejoices in the goodness of his God.

I was with him recently for a brief visit, during which time we spoke of our families, our work, imminent publication deadlines, and upcoming travel and conferences. When I needed to leave to catch a plane home, I began to gather my things. Before I could stand, however, Jim grabbed my hand, drew me back into my chair, and asked sweetly if he could offer a prayer as we parted. His prayer was tender and earnest, a petition that the Lord would help us in our weakness to be better men and that we would be magnified in our efforts to build up the kingdom of God. Then came what was for me the most moving part of the prayer—his expression of love for God and his undying gratitude for the redemption of Jesus Christ. I was in tears as we separated.

An attitude of gratitude is downright contagious. People who express sincere thanks, who acknowledge themselves as no more than a dim reflection of the lamp (Christ is the Light; see 3 Nephi 18:24), and who are eager to point others to the Source of their joy and strength—such persons are the kind of folks I love to be with. They bless lives by their very presence. It isn't what they *say* that makes such a difference but rather who and what they *are*.

For many years I wrestled with how to take a compliment. I don't know how many hundreds of talks or lessons I've given over the last thirty years, but it's been a lot. And more than once people have thanked me afterward. Their compliments have been as varied as the personalities of the people themselves. Some simply say, "Good job," or "Great talk," or "I really enjoyed your message." Other compliments take the form of follow-up questions, requests for clarification, or an eagerness to get a reference or source for a thought or quotation. As a speaker and teacher, I appreciate the effort they make to provide feedback.

For the longest time, however, I just didn't handle such compliments properly. I often said something like, "Oh, you don't mean that" or "Well, not really; I thought it was sort of mediocre" or "Thanks, but I only got through half of my material; I didn't really cover the topic well." My wife, Shauna, noticed my discomfort and suggested that I take a different approach: I might try saying, "Thank you." It actually works quite well.

In recent years I have discovered another way to handle compliments. I find myself saying things like, "Thank you. It *was* a great evening, wasn't it? The Lord was good to us" or "There *was* a sweet Spirit in our midst. I'm grateful I was here and able to participate in it." Those aren't just handy homilies to me, nor are they insincere. The longer I live and the more I experience, the more clearly I perceive the workings of the Lord; if we have an inspiring experience together, all of the glory and honor and thanks ought to go to God.

I still remember very distinctly the words of

President Joseph Fielding Smith at the April 1970 general conference, at which he was sustained as the tenth president of the Church. "I desire to say that no man of himself can lead this church," President Smith affirmed. "It is the Church of the Lord Jesus Christ; he is at the head. The Church bears his name, has his priesthood, administers his gospel, preaches his doctrine, and does his work.

"He chooses men and calls them to be instruments in his hands to accomplish his purposes, and he guides and directs them in their labors. But men are only instruments in the Lord's hands, and the honor and glory for all that his servants accomplish is and should be ascribed unto him forever" (Conference Report, April 1970, 113).

King Benjamin graciously counseled his people that if they have labored tirelessly to serve him, their earthly king, "then ought not ye to labor to serve one another?" He added that if the people felt any desire to render thanks to him, "O how you ought to thank your heavenly King!" Then flow these powerful words: "I say unto you, my brethren [and sisters], that if you should render all the thanks and praise which your whole soul has power to possess, to that God who has created you, and has kept and preserved you, . . .—I say unto you that if ye should serve him who has created you from the beginning, and is preserving you from day to day, by lending you breath, . . . and even supporting you from one moment to another—I say, *if ye should serve him with all your whole souls yet ye would be unprofitable servants*" (Mosiah 2:18–21; emphasis added).

What kind of message is that? Don't such sentiments create feelings of futility, an attitude of "What difference does it make?"

Not if we understand what Benjamin and the Savior himself taught during his mortal ministry (Luke 17:10). Rather, such words should create feelings of profound *humility,* feelings of gratitude, of reverence, of resounding praise to him who holds all things in his power and is the source of our strength and very being. This is what might be called the "doctrine of divine indebtedness." Elder Gerald N. Lund pointed out that "focusing on the word *profit* will help us better understand the concept of unprofitable servants. The word implies personal gain or benefit. *Profit* means an increase in assets or status or benefits.

"That is the crux of the concept of man being an unprofitable servant. God is perfect—in knowledge, power, influence, and attributes. He is the Creator of *all* things! What could any person—or all people together for that matter—do to bring profit (that is, an increase in assets, status, or benefits) to God? . . .

"That we are his children and he loves us is undeniable, and that situation puts us in a status far above any of his other creations. But *we must somehow disabuse ourselves of any notion that we can bring personal profit to God by our actions. That would make God indebted to men, which is unthinkable*" (*Jesus Christ, Key*, 120–21; emphasis added).

Are we there yet? Have we arrived at the point where we feel perfectly comfortable to climb into the celestial limousine and be chauffeured through the pearly gates? Probably not. But that's okay, as long as we have made the decision to follow Christ, come unto him, and pursue the path of the disciple (we call that the gospel covenant). At least we are headed in the right direction. To the extent that we realize who we are, Whose we are, what we can do, and what we can never, worlds without end, do for ourselves, our Heavenly Father and his Beloved Son will do everything in their power to forgive us, equip us, empower us, transform us, and ultimately glorify us.

We may not be there yet, but we're well on the way when we begin to acknowledge our limitations, confess his goodness and mercy and strength, and learn to embody an attitude of gratitude. In the language of the revelation, we are to "thank the Lord [our] God in all things" (D&C 59:7; see also v. 21). In weakness there is strength (2 Corinthians 12:9–10; Ether 12:27). In submission and surrender, there is power and victory. Thanks be to God, who grants us that victory through the mediation of his Son, the Lord Jesus Christ (1 Corinthians 15:57).

EIGHT

Chasing Darkness Away

WHILE I WAS SERVING AS STAKE president, a member of my stake came into my office for a temple recommend interview. I asked all the questions, and the person gave all the right answers. This member was worthy and virtuous to the core. There was a light in his countenance that comes only through sustained righteousness. At the end of the interview I commended him on his worthiness to enter the temple and asked, "And how are you doing overall?"

He responded with a sweet smile and said, "President Millet, I'm doing great! I feel so good about life. I haven't had to repent in months."

I was stunned by his words and said, "Wow, you *are* doing well. In fact, I don't think I've met anyone quite like you. How do you do it?"

What followed was a very productive conversation, one that was useful to the Church member and especially good for me. Clearly, what he intended to convey was that he had not needed to repent of any serious transgression. But I spoke with him about the fact that in a very real sense life is repentance; improvement is repentance; refinement is repentance. Repentance is something we ought to be involved with every day of our lives in constantly striving to put away the foolishness and froth of our fleeting world, in regularly seeking divine assistance to put off the natural man and put on Christ. Now, don't misunderstand. As the Prophet Joseph Smith pointed out, "Repentance is a thing that cannot be trifled with every day. Daily transgression and daily repentance is not that which is pleasing in the sight of God" (*Teachings of the Prophet Joseph Smith,* 148). My guess is that the Prophet was referring to committing the same sin again and again and going to the Lord frequently and repeatedly to plead for forgiveness.

God-fearing people live in a constant state of repentance, in that they are striving to maintain the influence of the Spirit in their lives and thus open themselves to its sanctifying power. The people of King Benjamin may have lost their desire to commit sin (Mosiah 5:1–2), but that doesn't mean they never sinned again; rather, they may have sinned, but *they didn't want to.* Their *disposition* had been changed.

"Will sin be perfectly destroyed?" President

Brigham Young asked. "No, it will not, for it is not so designed in the economy of heaven. . . . Do not suppose that we shall ever in the flesh be free from temptations to sin. Some suppose that they can in the flesh be sanctified body and spirit and become so pure that they will never again feel the effects of the power of the adversary of truth. Were it possible for a person to attain to this degree of perfection in the flesh, he could not die neither remain in a world where sin predominates. . . . I think we shall more or less feel the effects of sin so long as we live, and finally have to pass the ordeals of death" (*Journal of Discourses,* 10:173).

On another occasion President Young affirmed the mortal challenge: "It requires all the atonement of Christ, the mercy of the Father, the pity of angels and the grace of the Lord Jesus Christ to be with us always, and then to do the very best we possibly can, to get rid of this sin within us, so that we may escape from this world into the celestial kingdom" (*Journal of Discourses,* 11:301).

Repentance is a fascinating word, one whose linguistic origins teach us a great deal about the word's meaning. The Hebrew Old Testament word means "to turn"—to turn away from sin, to turn toward God. The Greek New Testament word means "to acquire a new way of seeing things," to have a "change of mind." When put together, the Old and New Testament words imply that repentance is associated with a change in one's direction or behavior as well as a change of one's thinking, feelings, and very being. Through the years, as I have worked with members of the Church in transgression, I have found that certain questions prove helpful in assessing the depth and sincerity of one's contrition and desire to change. Some of these are—

What is wrong with what you have done? Why is it so serious?

How do you feel about what you have done? Do you feel what you ought to feel? How do you think the Lord feels about it?

Are you prepared to put this out of your life and thereafter to put it behind you? Are you willing to commit (covenant) to the Lord, through his priesthood leader, that you have no intention whatsoever of doing this again? (Philippians 3:13–14).

Are you ready to "turn away" from your sins and begin to see things with new eyes and to feel things with a new heart? Are you prepared to do whatever is required of you to come back to the strait and narrow path? (Alma 22:15–18).

Are you prepared to undergo a complete change, to clean the whole house, as it were, and not just the living room? (Romans 12:1–3).

The Lord states that there are basically two aspects

of repentance: We must be willing to confess, and we must be willing to forsake (D&C 58:42–43). Has there been a full confession, a complete disclosure of the sin? What do you need to do to forsake your sins? Are you prepared to do so?

What are some things you need to do in the coming days and weeks to receive forgiveness of your sins? How about the following?

• Prayer (for forgiveness, for a changed heart, for strength to forsake; Psalm 51:1–4, 6–13, 16–17)

• Scripture study and reading good books (D&C 18:34–36; 88:118)

• Church attendance (Matthew 18:20; Alma 6:6; Moroni 6:5; D&C 20:75)

• Avoiding influences that degrade or weaken the resolve (certain music, movies, videos, pornography, or associations)

• Putting more and more light into our lives (inspiring music, general conference addresses, talk tapes, and so forth). These allow us to "chase darkness from among [us]" (D&C 50:25; see also v. 24).

How will you know when you are forgiven? How will you know when it is appropriate for you to regain the privileges of Church membership? (Mosiah 4:1–3; Alma 24:10).

What are some ways of knowing whether you have

undergone a "mighty change" of heart? (Mosiah 5:2). What must you do to stay clean, to retain a remission of sins? (Mosiah 4:11–12, 26; 5:1; 27:23–26; 28:3–4; Alma 5; 13:12; 19:33; 36; Galatians 5:22–25).

What is the relationship of the Savior's merits and mercy to the forgiveness of your sins? (1 Nephi 10:4–6; 2 Nephi 2:3–8; Alma 22:12–14; D&C 45:3–5).

I have come to believe that yesterday's weapons are not adequate in facing today's assaults. That is, inasmuch as today's allurements and temptations to sin are both stronger and more subtle than those of the past, it is in fact necessary for us to do everything we can to fill our minds and hearts with even greater amounts of light and truth. We must first be honest with ourselves and with God: Is this particular activity or association uplifting, edifying, approved of the Lord? What are some things in which I participate that have no place in the life of a man or woman seriously interested in spiritual things? What things simply have to go if I am to enjoy the lifting and cleansing and revelatory powers of the Spirit? What can be added to my life to strengthen and sustain my defense?

Because they are human, those who have walked in the light may step momentarily into the darkness. When they do so, they experience the pain and sense of alienation that accompany sin, and they are repulsed by those feelings. What is their greatest desire? To get back into the light and stay there. In that sense, those who have consciously decided to follow Christ and reject Satan learn to "speedily repent" (D&C 109:21) when they do step off the gospel path. Because they have been born of the Spirit, have come to cherish virtue and disdain evil, they cannot *continue* in sin (JST 1 John 3:9).

The gospel of Jesus Christ is a grand system of education—"the power of God unto salvation" (Romans 1:16) that educates our desires, educates our conscience, educates our feelings, educates our hopes and dreams, and thereby sanctifies the whole human soul. Our commission as Christians is to avoid being conformed to this world but rather to become transformed by the renewing of our minds (Romans 12:2), such that over time we gain "the mind of Christ" (1 Corinthians 2:16). As someone has said, Jesus came to earth to do more than make bad men good; he came to bring dead men back to life. And it is that life, the abundant life (John 10:10), that comes to us through being washed in the blood of the Lamb and enlivened by the power of his Spirit. Truly, as Paul wrote, Christ has abolished death and "brought life and immortality to light through the gospel" (2 Timothy 1:10). God be praised for the gift of repentance!

NINE

Truer Than True

ALTHOUGH WE ARE HERE ON EARTH to overcome the flesh and acquire, through the Atonement, a Christlike character, God does not expect us to work ourselves into spiritual, emotional, or physical oblivion. Nor does he desire that the members of the Church be truer than true. There is little virtue in excess, even in gospel excess. In fact, as we go beyond the established mark, we open ourselves to deception and ultimately to destruction. Imbalance leads to instability. If Satan cannot cause us to lie or steal or smoke or be immoral, it just may be that he will cause our strength—our zeal for goodness and righteousness—to become our weakness. He will encourage excess, for surely any virtue, when taken to the extreme, becomes a vice.

A friend of mine shared the following experience. More than forty years ago he and his wife became acquainted with an older couple in their ward. This couple was about as devoted to the Church as people could be. The wife had been raised in the Church, and her husband had come into contact with the missionaries and been baptized while in the military. Like most of us, this couple had had their ups and downs in the faith, had struggled with a commandment here and there, but had managed to put much of the foolishness of youth behind them. In their eagerness to "make up" for all the times they may have disappointed the Lord, they determined upon a course to do everything they could to live the laws of the gospel perfectly. They would leave no stone unturned, no "i" undotted. If the Lord through his Church asked for 10 percent of their income as a tithing, they would pay 15 percent. If Church members were asked to fast once per month, they would fast once per week. If most people studied the scriptures an hour per day, they would search and ponder and pray for two hours. And so on and so on.

Neighbors began to feel uncomfortable around them. The couple withdrew into themselves and away from others who did not share their zeal. It was only a matter of time before Satan capitalized on their imbalance and led them to the brink of spiritual destruction. Only through the love, patience, and vigilance of priesthood leaders, loved ones, and friends were they delivered from their precarious precipice and enabled to begin the slow and painful return to the true strait and narrow path.

In this case, and in too many others, persons who determine upon a course that will take them beyond the expected, above the required, inevitably begin to expect the same of others. It becomes a "religious" principle, one to which persons are proselytized. The overzealous tend to judge others by their own standard. One could take a simple observance, such as fasting or praying, and soon find, with just the slightest amount of extra zeal, that these wonderful principles, given for the blessing and benefit of humankind, contribute to error.

I spoke once to a temple president who described what had happened over the years in the temple in which he and his wife had presided. He said that there was a particular room set aside as a prayer room, a place where patrons of the temple could retire for pondering and meditation, to seek inspiration or guidance on personal matters. For the longest time, he said, the room served a useful purpose: It reminded the patrons that temples are places of learning and revelation, holy edifices where they attend to sacred matters for the living as well as the dead. In time, however, the room became such a popular spot that long lines often wound their way around the celestial room, where hosts of people stood waiting to get their turn.

"Sometimes," the former temple president said, "people went into the room, and we simply couldn't get them out. Some of them," he added, "would pray themselves into a frenzy."

Gospel hobbies lead to imbalance. To instability. To distraction. To misperception. They are dangerous and should be avoided as we would any other sin. President Joseph F. Smith said: "We frequently look about us and see people who incline to extremes, who are fanatical. We may be sure that this class of people do not understand the gospel. They have forgotten, if they ever knew, that it is very unwise to take a fragment of truth and treat it as if it were the whole thing" (*Gospel Doctrine,* 122). To ride a gospel hobby is to participate in and perpetuate fanaticism. Harsh words, but true ones.

On another occasion President Smith taught: "Brethren and sisters, don't have hobbies. Hobbies are dangerous in the Church of Christ. They are dangerous because they give undue prominence to certain principles or ideas to the detriment and dwarfing of others just as important, just as binding, just as saving as the favored doctrines or commandments.

"Hobbies give to those who encourage them a false

aspect of the gospel of the Redeemer; they distort and place out of harmony its principles and teachings. The point of view is unnatural. Every principle and practice revealed from God is essential to man's salvation, and to place any one of them unduly in front, hiding and dimming all others is unwise and dangerous; it jeopardizes our salvation, for it darkens our minds and beclouds our understandings. . . .

"We have noticed this difficulty: that Saints with hobbies are prone to judge and condemn their brethren and sisters who are not so zealous in the one particular direction of their pet theory as they are. . . . There is another phase of this difficulty—the man with a hobby is apt to assume an 'I am holier than thou' position, to feel puffed up and conceited, and to look with distrust, if with no severer feeling, on his brethren and sisters who do not so perfectly live that one particular law" (*Gospel Doctrine*, 116–17).

True excellence in gospel living—compliance with the established laws and ordinances in a quiet and consistent and patient manner—results in humility, in greater reliance upon God, and a broadening love and acceptance of one's fellowman.

There is a principle here: What I am doing in the name of goodness ought to bring me closer to those I love and serve, ought to turn my heart toward people rather than cause me to turn my nose up in judgmental rejection. The greatest Man to walk the earth, the only fully perfect human being, looked with tenderness and compassion upon those whose ways and actions were less than perfect. His is the example.

In short, we have been counseled to stay in the mainstream of the Church, to see to it that our obedience and faithfulness reflect sane and balanced living. While we are to be true, we need not be truer than true. While we are not to partake of the vices of the world, we are to live in it. While we are to be "valiant in the testimony of Jesus" (D&C 76:79), we are not to be excessive in our zeal. We will arrive safely at the end of our gospel journey through steady and dedicated discipleship—loving and trusting the Lord, keeping his commandments, and serving his children—not through crusades or marathons. True conversion manifests itself in settled simplicity.

TEN

"Forgetting Those Things Which Are Behind"

I HAD BEEN ON MY MISSION for only a few days when my companion and I focused that day's study period on scriptural references to repentance. After we had read and discussed each of the passages, my companion—a very distinguished and polished elder, one who had been out eight months longer than I— said to me, "Just keep this in mind, Elder Millet: If you can still remember your sins, then that's evidence that God has not forgiven you."

I thought perhaps I had misunderstood what he said, and I asked, "What's that again?"

"If you can still remember sins you committed in the past," he stated with great firmness, "then the Lord has not forgiven you."

I asked timidly, "Is that right? Are you sure?"

He responded boldly and confidently. "That's what the scriptures teach. I'm just telling you the way it is."

I can still remember (now almost forty years later) the conflicting feelings in my heart and the racing thoughts in my head. I could recall, without really trying hard, many, many of my sins. With vividness. In Technicolor. Consequently, I went into a mild depression for about two weeks, conscious that whatever sins I had committed during my life that were still hanging around the edges of memory were undealt with. I was one sinful and guilty character!

There was only one problem with what my companion taught me, even though I am sure he meant well. The major flaw in his thinking was this: It was wrong! As I browsed the scriptures on my own in the weeks following his devastating statement, it became clear to me that certain pretty significant people—Saul of Tarsus and Alma the Younger, for example—still remembered their sins, long after they had been committed, repented of, and forgiven. What the Lord had indeed taught in scripture was not that *we* would forget our sins but that *he remembered them no more* once we had fully repented of them (D&C 58:42–43). What a difference.

There is a sense in which life and death are defined in terms of one another. In a way, we must die as pertaining to premortality in order to be born into mortality. We must die here as pertaining to sin and evil in order to be born unto righteousness. We must die as pertaining to mortality in order to be born unto immortality and eternal life. We must be born. We must die. That is the plan.

"Know ye not," the apostle Paul wrote, "that so many of us as were baptized into Jesus Christ were baptized into his death?" That is, to be baptized unto Christ is to participate in and incorporate his atonement by symbolic action. We go down into the watery grave and come forth unto new life, new life in Christ. "Therefore we are buried with him by baptism into death: that like as Christ was raised up from the dead by the glory of the Father, even so we also should walk in newness of life" (Romans 6:3–4).

The Messiah needed to die before he could be quickened (John 12:24). So too with us. We must put to death the old person of sin in order to be transformed, to be quickened by the power of God. Then we walk in newness of life.

"For if we have been planted together in the likeness of his death," Paul continued, "we shall be also in the likeness of his resurrection" (Romans 6:5). Another translation of this passage renders it: "For if we have become *identified with him* in his death, we shall also be identified with him in his resurrection" (Revised English Bible; emphasis added). Truly, in the life to come we will come forth from the grave as Christ the Firstfruits has shown us. In addition, those who come unto Christ with full purpose of heart in this life, who "offer [their] whole souls as an offering unto him" (Omni 1:26), who sacrifice the natural man on the altar of redemption, are quickened, made alive to the things of the Spirit. In summary, the execution of the will of our Lord and Master in our lives requires the execution of our old self and the birth of a new person.

"The more you obey your conscience," C. S. Lewis stated, "the more your conscience will demand of you. And your natural self, which is thus being starved and hampered and worried at every turn, will get angrier and angrier. In the end, you will either give up trying to be good, or else become one of those people who, as they say, 'live for others' but always in a discontented, grumbling way. . . .

"The Christian way is different: harder, and easier. Christ says 'Give me All. I don't want so much of your time and so much of your money and so much of your work: *I want You. I have not come to torment your natural self, but to kill it.* No half-measures are any good. I don't want to cut off a branch here and a branch there, I want to have the whole tree down. I don't want to drill the tooth, or crown it, or stop it, but to have it out. *Hand over the whole natural self,* all the desires which you think innocent as well as the ones you think wicked—the whole outfit. *I will give you a new self instead. In fact, I will give you Myself: my own will shall become yours*" (*Mere Christianity,* 169; emphasis added).

To have *put on Christ,* to have come unto him, is to have *put off the natural man* and to have opened ourselves to a new creation. This is, in fact, what is meant by the word *baptism.* The words *bapto* or *baptizo* did indeed have to do with immersion, and, more specifically, what something is like after it has been immersed. If we immerse a white cloth in scarlet dye, we could say that the cloth has been baptized; it has been immersed and has come forth with a new identity. It is like a new cloth.

We do not dwell on what or who we once were, for we have been changed. We are a new creation, a new creature in Christ. "This one thing I do," Paul wrote to another group of Saints, "*forgetting those things which are behind, and reaching forth unto those things which are before,* I press toward the mark for the prize of the high calling of God in Christ Jesus" (Philippians 3:13–14; emphasis added).

We as mortals simply do not have the power to fix everything that is broken. Complete restitution, as we know it, may not be possible. President Boyd K. Packer explained that "sometimes you *cannot* give back what you have taken because you don't have it to give. If you have caused others to suffer unbearably—defiled someone's virtue, for example—it is not within your power to give it back. . . .

"If you cannot undo what you have done, you are trapped. It is easy to understand how helpless and hopeless you then feel and why you might want to give up, just as Alma did.

"The thought that rescued Alma, when he acted upon it, is this: *Restoring what you cannot restore, healing the wound you cannot heal, fixing that which you broke and you cannot fix is the very purpose of the atonement of Christ.*

"When your desire is firm and you are willing to pay the 'uttermost farthing' [see Matthew 5:25–26], the law of restitution is suspended. *Your obligation is transferred to the Lord.* He will settle your accounts" (Conference Report, October 1995, 22–23; emphasis added).

The story is told of a woman who visited President Joseph Fielding Smith. She had been guilty of serious transgression but had fully repented and now just wanted to find her way. She had great difficulty forgiving herself, even though she had complied with the laws and principles of repentance. President Smith asked her to read to him from Genesis the story of the destruction of Sodom and Gomorrah and of Lot's wife being turned to a pillar of salt. He asked her what lesson was to be learned. She answered, tearfully, "The message of that story is that God will destroy the wicked." "Not so," President Smith told this repentant woman. "The message for you is: *'Don't look back!'*" (cited in Packer, "Fountain of Life").

I am afraid that too often we are much harsher judges of our actions and deeds than the Almighty would ever be. It seems to me that we need to pray without ceasing to be endowed with the spirit of mercy, with that spirit that would cause us to see our brothers and sisters—and ourselves—as God sees us. We need to pray without ceasing to be filled with charity, the pure love of Christ, so that we may feel toward our brothers and sisters—and ourselves—as God does. We need to pray that God will bless us to feel what we ought to feel. I certainly don't want to feel any more guilt than I should, but then I don't want to feel any less, either. Truly, "if our heart condemn us, God is greater than our heart, and knoweth all things" (1 John 3:20).

We need to learn to trust God's elevated perspective and his judgment more than we trust our own. In time, and through the quiet but steady workings of the Holy Spirit, our condemning heart will give way to mercy, will open itself to holy love, will enable us to see and feel things as they really are.

ELEVEN

Temple Living

IT SEEMS REASONABLE TO SUGGEST that the closer we get to our spiritual destination—the nearer we get to the Lord and the more settled we are in his kingdom—the more prominent the temple will become in our personal lives. Other than the home, the temple is the most sacred place on earth, a place to which we feel drawn as we mature in our faith. Elder Marion D. Hanks stated: "As the mission of the Church is to 'invite all to come unto Christ,' so I believe, in its clearest and loveliest sense, that this is *also the mission of temples,* where we not only undertake the sacred service of work for redemption of the dead, to open the door for them, but where the choicest of all opportunities exists to learn of Christ, and to come to know him and commune with him and to purify our own hearts" (cited in Nibley, *Temples of the Ancient World,* 16).

Salvation is in Christ. The temple is his house of learning, of communion and inspiration, of covenants and ordinances, of service, and of personal refinement. The temple is the house of the Lord. But it is not the Lord. We look to Christ the Person for salvation.

I have heard members of the Church say, "I never go to the temple without learning something, without gaining some new insight."

I wish I could say that, but I cannot. I have been to the temple hundreds and hundreds of times, and I have indeed learned a great deal, but not every time. I *can* say this, however: I have never been to the temple and not been blessed by the experience. I have never attended without coming away rewarded and deeply grateful for the Spirit I felt there, the sweet reminder of what matters most, and a stronger resolve to be loyal to the Lord and true to my covenants. I have gone there with serious financial worries on my mind. I don't remember ever coming out with more money in my pocket, but I have left with the peaceful assurance that God is in his heaven, that he knows my concerns, and that I need not fret over a matter unduly. I have gone into the temple particularly concerned about a wandering child. I do not remember ever returning home to find that our wanderer had come back having undergone a rapid, miraculous transformation. I have come home, however, comforted in the assurance that God is the Father of my child and that he has known and loved that child far longer than I have. In short, my soul has been comforted in Christ.

Because the temple is an earthly type of paradise, the postmortal abode of the faithful, I believe the words of Alma about paradise are applicable to the temple. The temple is a place where we enjoy "a state of rest, a state of peace, where [we] shall rest from all [our] troubles and from all care, and sorrow" (Alma 40:12). In that spirit, I have found myself reflecting again and again upon the counsel of President Howard W. Hunter:

"I invite the Latter-day Saints to look to the temple of the Lord as the great symbol of your membership. It is the deepest desire of my heart to have every member of the Church worthy to enter the temple. It would please the Lord if every adult member would be worthy of—and carry—a current temple recommend. The things that we must do and not do to be worthy of a temple recommend are the very things that ensure we will be happy as individuals and as families" (Conference Report, October 1994, 8).

On those occasions when we find ourselves taking our spiritual temperature, when we ask ourselves, "Are we there yet?" it might be helpful (and should be comforting) to realize that if we qualify to enter the house of the Lord, we qualify for life in paradise after death and the celestial kingdom after the resurrection.

You might respond, "But I'm far from perfect. I have a long way to go."

I reply, "Welcome to mortality. Welcome to earth. Welcome to the world of imperfect beings. Welcome to school. We are here *to prepare* for hereafter." As Amulek proclaimed, "This life is the time for men to prepare to meet God; yea, behold the day of this life is the day for men to perform their labors" (Alma 34:32).

"Those who put themselves in [God's] hands," C. S. Lewis reminds us, "will become perfect, as He is perfect—perfect in love, wisdom, joy, beauty, and immortality. The change will not be completed in this life, for death is an important part of the treatment" (*Mere Christianity,* 177). Or, as Joseph Smith explained, "When you climb up a ladder, you must begin at the bottom, and ascend step by step, until you arrive at the top; and so it is with the principles of the Gospel—you must begin with the first, and go on until you learn all the principles of exaltation. But it will be a great while after you have passed through the veil before you will have learned them. It is not all to be comprehended in this world; it will be a great work to learn our salvation and exaltation even beyond the grave" (*Teachings of the Prophet Joseph Smith,* 348).

So take heart. We are all in this together. Not one of us is as ready and prepared to face death as we would like to be, but we're on course; we're in the gospel harness; we're on track. And for now, that's all that matters.

TWELVE

Staying Clean

THE ODDS ARE PRETTY HIGH that we as mortals have committed at least one sin in our lives (some may even have slipped twice!). As my friend Sheri Dew has pointed out, sin makes us stupid, and it costs a lot, too (*No One Can Take Your Place,* 101). Why, then, would we choose to sin? Why would we do things that are stupid and that cost—in time, energy, and feelings of worth?

Some may sin through ignorance. Much of the time, however, we know exactly what we are doing—or at least we think we do. The fact is, if we really knew what we were doing, we'd do things the Lord's way and avoid the stupid distraction and dilution of our discipleship that sin proves to be. But part of being mortal is being nearsighted for a season. Part of growing up spiritually is learning to focus, to see the truth, to acquire the big picture, the distant vision.

While everyone makes mistakes and commits sin, not everyone wants to stay sinful. Most want to change, to be better, to do better. We call that change repentance. We call the result of true repentance forgiveness. Forgiveness is in every way a miracle, a phenomenal happening that makes each of us into a different person, a person who is pure and clean. Those who are striving to overcome evil and put sin out of their life know that forgiveness is an act of mercy on the part of a benevolent God, a gracious gift that we could never generate or create on our own. Forgiveness is a work of God.

During the years that I served as a bishop and stake president, it was not uncommon to hear the following questions from Church members in the process of having their sins remitted through proper repentance: "How do I know when my sin is gone? How will I know when I have been forgiven? When can I stop repenting of this particular sin and move on?"

These are important questions, questions that evidence that each of us desires comfort more than unrest, consolation rather than confusion, peace rather than distress and angst within our soul. The scriptures provide our best answers to these questions. For example, after King Benjamin had delivered a powerful sermon to his people on service, divine indebtedness, and putting off the natural man, the multitude fell to the earth, "for the fear of the Lord had come upon them." Acknowledging that they were unworthy before their Maker—indeed, "they had viewed themselves in their own carnal state, even less than the dust of the earth"— they cried unto the heavens for mercy and for the atoning blood of Christ to be applied to their souls. Then "after they had spoken these words *the Spirit of the Lord came upon them, and they were filled with joy,* having received a remission of their sins, and *having peace of conscience,* because of the exceeding faith which they had in Jesus Christ who should come" (Mosiah 4:1–3; emphasis added).

When I have studied these verses with university students, I have always asked how Benjamin's people knew they had been forgiven. The students fire back: "They felt joy" and "They felt peace of conscience." These answers are certainly correct. Joy is a fruit of the Spirit (Galatians 5:22), a feeling and an attribute that manifest that things are as they should be within us.

Peace of conscience is that glorious state in which we are no longer plagued by our sins. We may still remember them, but we do not remember them in the same way (Alma 36:19). Though we may be able to recall our sinful deeds, we no longer feel punished by them; we no longer feel the need to browbeat ourselves over them. Why? Because that was before and this is now. Because I am a different person now, a new creation of the Holy Ghost. I don't feel the need to rehash and relive my mistakes often any more than I feel the need to disinter the dead.

I generally follow up those answers by asking, "Any other clues to whether or when our sins are forgiven?"

There is usually an uncomfortable silence in the room as everyone looks again at the opening verses of Mosiah 4. What seems to be missed almost every time is something that is actually quite obvious, and perhaps the students simply assume it. It is this: "The Spirit of the Lord came upon them" (Mosiah 4:3).

Now if, as we understand, sin leads to a withdrawal of the Lord's Spirit (Alma 34:35; D&C 19:20), what does it mean when that Spirit returns? If the Spirit cannot abide in an unclean tabernacle, what do we conclude when that Spirit begins to abide with us once again? Simply stated, we are no longer unclean! The sin is gone. It is time to move on. One of the most important roles that priesthood leaders, specifically common judges, fulfill is bringing closure to cases of serious transgression. That is, it is their task to study and discern how the individual is progressing, to offer specific counsel and follow up on assignments, and to acknowledge when the Spirit has returned, thus signifying that the person is no longer under condemnation but has been forgiven.

There is nothing quite like being clean, of feeling pure and innocent as a little child. It is a state that each of us would fight to maintain, if we could. In fact, there have been times when, having experienced a remission of sins, I wanted nothing more than to stay that way, to avoid sin in all of its myriad manifestations, to climb into a plastic bubble and keep myself from further taint.

That's one approach, I suppose, but it's not very practical. How, then, can we stay clean? Having *obtained* a remission of sins, how do we then *retain* that state from day to day? How do we remain justified, innocent, exonerated? Is it even possible?

The scriptures joyously proclaim that there is a way. In fact, it is from Benjamin himself that we learn two valuable paths to retaining a remission of sins. First, Benjamin explains to his people that "as ye have come to the knowledge of the glory of God, or if ye have known of his goodness and have tasted of his love, and have received a remission of your sins, which causeth such exceedingly great joy in your souls, even so *I would that ye should remember, and always retain in remembrance, the greatness of God, and your own nothingness, and his goodness and long-suffering towards you, unworthy creatures, and humble yourselves even in the depths of humility, calling on the name of the Lord daily,* and standing steadfastly in the faith of that which is to come, which was spoken by the mouth of the angel" (Mosiah 4:11).

Benjamin then adds: "And behold, I say unto you that if ye do this ye shall always rejoice, and be filled with the love of God, and *always retain a remission of your sins:* and ye shall grow in the knowledge of the glory of him that created you, or in the knowledge of that which is just and true" (Mosiah 4:12; emphasis added).

It may not be obvious what is involved here. One of the keys to remaining unspotted from the sins of the world is to live in a constant state of humility, a state in which we repeatedly defer to God, acknowledge his goodness and majesty, recognize our absolute inability to make progress in life without him, and, as Alma later explained to Shiblon, "acknowledge [our] unworthiness before God at all times" (Alma 38:14). Pride or self-conceit is, as C. S. Lewis pointed out, "the essential vice, the utmost evil.

"Unchastity, anger, greed, drunkenness, and all that, are mere fleabites in comparison: it was through Pride that the devil became the devil: *Pride leads to every other vice:* it is the complete anti-God state of mind" (*Mere Christianity,* 109–10; emphasis added).

Thus, the way to keep ourselves outside the reach of Lucifer is to cultivate and maintain an attitude of gratitude, an outlook of total dependence upon Deity, a recognition that only in the strength of the Lord can we accomplish the Lord's purposes for us and thereby fulfill the measure of our creation (Philippians 4:13; Alma 26:12).

Benjamin's sermon speaks at length of our Christian covenantal obligation toward all men and women, especially those who are less fortunate than we are. He warns us about judging unrighteously or attributing unkind motivation to the beggars of this world: "For behold, are we not all beggars? Do we not all depend upon the same Being, even God, for all the substance which we have . . . ?" (Mosiah 4:19).

The noble king follows with these words, words that point up a second but related means of staying clean: "And now, for the sake of these things which I have spoken unto you—that is, *for the sake of retaining a remission of your sins from day to day, that ye may walk guiltless before God—I would that ye should impart of your substance to the poor,* every man according to that which he hath, such as feeding the hungry, clothing the naked, visiting the sick and administering to their relief, both spiritually and temporally, according to their wants" (Mosiah 4:26; emphasis added).

Caring for other people, shifting our glance from ourselves to our brothers and sisters, and learning to live outside ourselves are the kinds of attitudes and actions that steel us against sin and rivet us to righteousness. Benjamin himself taught that when we are in the service of our fellow beings we are only in the service of our God (Mosiah 2:17). This principle has powerful implications: One of the few ways we can serve God is through serving others. Being involved in the work of the Master, the work of lifting and feeding and healing, brings to us the blessings of the Master.

A friend shared with me that many years ago he attended a stake priesthood leadership meeting at which Elder Bruce R. McConkie presided. After speaking to the group for a while, Elder McConkie invited questions. One man asked what must have seemed at the time to be a rather broad question: "What can we do to guarantee that we will inherit eternal life?"

My friend indicated that Elder McConkie didn't even pause but said firmly: "Take the sacrament worthily every week."

Of course! If we live in a state of humility and repentance; if we see to it that our lives are in harmony with the teachings of the scriptures, the prophets, and the Church; and if we repair to our sacrament meetings in an attitude of worship and reverence and submission, then surely the day will come when the Lord God will say to us, "Thou shalt be exalted."

The risen Lord declared to the Nephites that those who have come unto the gospel covenant, who repent and are baptized, "shall be filled; and *if he endureth to the end, behold, him will I hold guiltless before my Father* at that day when I shall stand to judge the world" (3 Nephi 27:16; emphasis added).

Remorse will be gone. Guilt will be no more. Joy and peace will preside.

THIRTEEN

"Come Boldly unto the Throne of Grace"

IT'S ONE THING TO ASK, "Are we there yet?" and quite another to ask, "Am I really ready to arrive?" One can speed down the highway, run red lights, and throw caution to the wind to arrive at a business meeting on time but still be unprepared for the meeting. Getting there is one thing; feeling comfortable at the destination is another thing entirely. In a spiritual vein, there are those who want to specialize in the signs of the times: They have immersed themselves in beasts and numbers and astral phenomena and warnings and plagues. But the real question is not when the Second Coming will be, but rather, will we be ready to greet the Lord when he returns in glory?

"To come out of the world," President Stephen L Richards observed, "one must forsake the philosophy of the world, and to come into Zion one must adopt the philosophy of Zion. In my own thinking I have reduced the process to a very simple formula: Forsake the philosophy of self-sufficiency, which is the philosophy of the world, and adopt the philosophy of faith, which is the philosophy of Christ. Substitute faith for self-assurance" (*Where Is Wisdom?* 419).

If during this life our trust and reliance have been upon ourselves—in our accomplishments, our plaudits, our earthly rewards—then we will fall far short of what could have been ours in eternity had we learned to lean upon the ample arm of Jehovah.

If, on the other hand, we have learned the lesson of the ages—that without faith it is impossible to please God (Hebrews 11:6) and that with faith all things can be accomplished—then we will not only be on that path that leads to life eternal but ready and prepared to go there and comfortable in dwelling there forever.

Consider the remarkable testimony of Enos, son of Jacob: "I soon go to the place of my rest, which is with my Redeemer; for I know that in him I shall rest. And I rejoice in the day when my mortal shall put on immortality, and shall stand before him; *then shall I see his face with pleasure,* and he will say unto me: Come unto me, ye blessed, there is a place prepared for you in the mansions of my Father" (Enos 1:27; emphasis added).

I believe Enos was a righteous and noble man, but I do not believe he was without flaw or weakness. I believe he endured faithfully to the end, but I doubt he did everything just the way he might have wished he had done it. His confidence and pleasure in being welcomed into the presence of the Lord Omnipotent did not derive from his personal goodness alone but also (and perhaps more importantly) from his full acceptance of the Atonement and his total trust that Jesus Christ could and would do all he had promised.

Let's repeat what we pointed out earlier: Grace represents God's acceptance of me. Faith represents my acceptance of God's acceptance of me. Peace is my acceptance of me.

John the Beloved counseled us: "And now, little children, abide in [Christ]; that, when he shall appear, we may have confidence, and not be ashamed before him at his coming" (1 John 2:28).

"Beloved, if our heart condemn us not, then have we confidence toward God. And whatsoever we ask, we receive of him, because we keep his commandments, and do those things that are pleasing in his sight" (1 John 3:21–22).

"And this is the confidence that we have in him, that, if we ask any thing according to his will, he heareth us" (1 John 5:14).

Similarly, the Prophet Joseph wrote under inspiration in the Liberty Jail that to the extent we seek to lead others through the divine pattern of persuasion, long-suffering, gentleness and meekness, love unfeigned, kindness, pure knowledge, divine reproof, charity, and virtue, "*then shall [our] confidence wax strong in the presence of God;* and the doctrine of the priesthood shall distil upon [our] soul as the dews from heaven. The Holy Ghost shall be [our] constant companion, and [our] scepter an unchanging scepter of righteousness and truth; and [our] dominion shall be an everlasting dominion, and without compulsory means it shall flow unto [us] forever and ever" (D&C 121:41–46; emphasis added).

President David O. McKay taught that spirituality was "the consciousness of victory over self, and of communion with the Infinite" (*Gospel Ideals,* 390). With trust in the Savior and the attendant righteousness that flows therefrom, we receive a quiet but steadying confidence, an assurance, a knowledge that the course in life we are pursuing is according to the will of God (Smith, *Lectures on Faith,* 3:5). Such confidence, like the love of God, casts out all fear (1 John 4:18; Moroni 8:16).

This confidence is no more nor less than a ripened faith, a faith that gives birth to hope. "Seeing then that we have a great high priest, that is passed into the heavens, Jesus the Son of God, let us hold fast our profession. For we have not an high priest which cannot be touched with the feeling of our infirmities; but was in all points tempted like as we are, yet without sin. *Let us therefore come boldly unto the throne of grace, that we may obtain mercy, and find grace to help in time of need"* (Hebrews 4:14–16; emphasis added).

The New American Standard Bible renders this last verse as follows: "Therefore let us draw near with confidence to the throne of grace, so that we may receive mercy and find grace to help in time of need." Another modern rendering of the Bible expresses the thought: "We don't have a priest who is out of touch with our reality. He's been through weakness and testing, experienced it all—all but the sin. So let's walk right up to him and get what he is so ready to give. Take the mercy, accept the help" (The Message).

Thus, when we have had faith, received hope, and come to know the surpassing love of God, fear and apprehension and discomfort flee.

To fear God is to reverence him, to respect him, to worship him. Being frightened or horrified of God leads to anxiety and worry and thus to counterproductive living, as we see in the parable of the talents in Matthew 25. On the other hand, faith and faithfulness lead to confidence and appropriate boldness in the presence of Deity. "Forasmuch as thou art God," Enoch addressed the Almighty, "and I know thee, and thou hast sworn unto me, and commanded me that I should ask in the name of thine Only Begotten; *thou hast made me, and given unto me a right to thy throne, and not of myself, but through thine own grace*" (Moses 7:59; emphasis added).

As followers of the Christ, we have the right to call upon the Father in the name of the Son, to one day come into their presence calmly and confidently, and to enjoy thereafter everlasting love and fellowship with those we worship (1 John 1:3). We will have come home. And we will feel safe and secure in the eternal family of God forevermore.

FOURTEEN

From Rules to Real Religion

MANY YEARS AGO CHARLES SHELDON wrote a novel that has become a classic Christian bestseller. The story, *In His Steps,* is about a Protestant minister who takes seriously the injunction to emulate the life of the one sinless soul ever to walk the earth. He determined that he would ask himself, whenever a decision was needed, "What would Jesus do?" Further, he extended the invitation to his congregation to do the same. It is a touching and poignant drama about the challenges one faces when he or she takes seriously the invitation to follow Christ. How does such a covenant affect the kinds of entertainment I allow in my business establishment? How does this commitment affect the kinds of articles I allow to be printed in my magazine? How does it affect my decision to open my business on the Sabbath? And so forth.

Again and again the leaders of our Church have

charged us as Latter-day Saints to do this very thing—to ask ourselves, "What would Jesus do?" and then to have the courage to follow where he leads. In fact, this very commission is as old as the world (Moses 5:5–8).

Nephi also encouraged us to "press forward with a steadfastness in Christ, having a perfect brightness of hope, and a love of God and of all men. Wherefore, if ye shall press forward, *feasting upon the word of Christ, and endure to the end,* behold, thus saith the Father: Ye shall have eternal life" (2 Nephi 31:20; emphasis added).

It is of interest to me that Nephi added the injunction to "[feast] upon the word of Christ" to the injunction to "endure to the end." In my mind this is not insignificant, for it points toward how we come to know what Jesus would do. We endure to the end faithfully by living as Jesus would live. But how do we know how Jesus would do things?

We can search the scriptures, a priceless collection of the words of Christ. We can study his life and ministry, noting how he dealt with friends, how he dealt with enemies and with difficulty, how he dealt with praise and adoration, how he taught the gospel. And yet all of these teachings—more precious than silver and gold—are not sufficient to cover every exigency, every possible aspect of our lives. It would not be long before we found ourselves in a real-life situation in which we could identify no close parallel in the life and ministry of Christ or the teachings of his authorized servants. What do we do then? How do we proceed? How do we do what Jesus would do if it is not recorded in sacred scripture or the counsel of prophets?

Again we turn to Nephi for direction: "And now, behold, my beloved brethren, I suppose that *ye ponder somewhat in your hearts concerning that which ye should do after ye have entered in by the way.* But, behold, why do ye ponder these things in your hearts? . . .

" . . . Wherefore, I said unto you, *feast upon the words of Christ; for behold, the words of Christ will tell you all things what ye should do.*

"Wherefore, now after I have spoken these words, if ye cannot understand them it will be because ye ask not, neither do ye knock; wherefore, ye are not brought into the light, but must perish in the dark.

"For behold, again I say unto you that *if ye will enter in by the way, and receive the Holy Ghost, it will show unto you all things what ye should do*" (2 Nephi 32:1–5; emphasis added).

There is our answer. We endure faithfully to the end by cultivating the gift of the Holy Ghost in our lives. We know how Jesus would speak or act under this or that circumstance by inspiration, through the direction of the Spirit, that third member of the Godhead who will *tell* and *show* us how to proceed.

We cannot exist on written scripture alone, nor can we survive in a wicked world with the added benefit of prophetic declarations, handbooks, and resource manuals. The strength of this Church is to be found in the hearts and lives of its individual members, in the manner in which they seek for and obtain the mind of God through the instrumentality of the Holy Spirit. Ours is the privilege of partaking of the fruit of a living tree of life, to be governed by a living constitution. "Notwithstanding those things which are written," the Lord declared in a modern revelation, "it always has been given to the elders of my church from the beginning, and ever shall be, to conduct all meetings as they are directed and guided by the Holy Spirit" (D&C 46:2; see also Moroni 6:9; D&C 20:45).

The Church generally seeks to teach us guiding principles, but quite often it is the Holy Ghost who will teach us specific practices.

Many years ago while serving as a counselor in a stake presidency, I temporarily assumed the leadership of the stake when the president left the country for an extended period. On one of the first Sabbath evenings after the president left, the phone rang. It was one of the bishops, who called with a question.

"President Millet," he said, "I have a couple in my ward who have been planning for several months to be married in the temple. I just discovered in a recent interview with them that a problem has arisen." Then he mentioned the specific matter.

I said, "Bishop, you know what we have been counseled to do when those particular sins occur, don't you?"

He stated that he knew what we generally did but asked, "President, would you be willing to meet with this couple?"

I indicated that I would be happy to meet with them but that such was unnecessary, given the nature of the offense and the instructions the stake presidency had given to the bishops.

"I understand," he replied, "but would you be willing to meet with them anyway?"

It seemed clear to me that this bishop was pushing his responsibilities off on me, but I gave in and agreed to meet with them the next day at 5:30 P.M.

It would be an immense understatement to say that my interview with the couple was not what I had expected. I confess that I went into the meeting with an agenda, with a planned outline of what would be said and what would be done. I knew the offense, and I knew what we had always done about it in the past. I had anticipated that they would be upset because the temple marriage would need to be postponed, and I would have bet my life that there would be a bit of defiance in their attitudes.

What I found, however, were two beautiful young people in the depths of humility, individuals who had spent the last several days pleading with the Lord for forgiveness and who were resigned to the fact that what they had so looked forward to was not to be, at least for now.

The young man spoke for both of them. "President Millet, we only want to do what the Lord would have us do. We are prepared to receive whatever discipline is appropriate. We know clearly that what we have done is a serious offense, one that cannot be ignored. We don't want to go into the temple unworthily."

I was stunned. Neither their verbal response to the sin nor their countenances were what I had imagined I would encounter. I was completely honest with the couple and told them that I frankly did not know what should be done.

My suggestion was that we pray together about the matter. We knelt, and the young man prayed first, then the young woman, and then myself. There was a simplicity in their voices, a pleading that was borne of the Spirit, a longing that bespoke the fact that they had indeed experienced what the scriptures call a broken heart and a contrite spirit. While the young woman was praying, there came into my mind the words of President Spencer W. Kimball that some people can repent more in twenty-four hours than others can in twenty-four months.

I knew by what I had heard and by what I felt that their hearts and their lives had truly been changed and their whole-souled offering accepted by God. We arose from prayer and wiped our eyes. I said, "I feel, and the Spirit seems to accord, that you should go ahead with your temple plans." Many more tears flowed as we separated.

After they left my office, I sat at my desk for quite some time. Mixed feelings filled my soul. I was thrilled for the couple and rejoiced in the goodness of God. On the other hand, I felt chastened severely by the Lord and his Spirit. Though there were no words spoken to me, it was as though God had said, "You listen to me: *This is my Church,* and these are my children. I alone know the hearts of men and women. If you are going to represent me, you had better humble yourself, open yourself to my guidance, and avoid trying to lead the people from some preconceived notions you may have. Repent!"

It was a terribly sobering moment for me, one for

which I am extremely grateful. I am also—more so now than ever before—eternally grateful that even the least of us can know what Jesus would do by importuning the Father in prayer.

I hasten to add that their transgression had not been so serious that they would automatically have disqualified themselves from participating in the ordinances of the house of the Lord, but it was such that a decision needed to be made. I am one who is committed to following the rules and regulations and guidelines laid down by the leaders of the Church; otherwise, we would spread chaos in the kingdom. And yet, no two cases are exactly the same, nor do any two people have identical needs. God deals with us "one by one," hearing our personal prayers and sending forth succor and relief, all according to our unique circumstances.

A dear friend of mine is an Evangelical Christian pastor. As we were first getting to know one another, Greg and I went to lunch often, spent hours in doctrinal discussion, and plumbed the depths of the differences between our two faiths. Over the years we have come to appreciate some meaningful similarities in our views on the central core doctrine of Christ, while at the same time continuing our discussions about our differences. Early in this process, my friend said to me during a discussion on how salvation comes: "But, Bob, you people have to do so many things to be saved."

"Like what?" I asked.

"Oh, you know. You need to read scriptures, go to church, pay tithing, go home teaching, go to the temple, and do scads of other things."

I thought for a moment before I spoke. Then I asked, "Greg, do you read the scriptures?"

He gave me a funny look and replied, "Of course I read the scriptures; I'm a minister."

I followed up with, "Why do you read the scriptures?"

He answered, "Because they feed my soul. They fill me with light and understanding. It's a significant part of my daily devotions and worship of God."

I said, "I read the scriptures, too. I suppose there was a time, perhaps twenty or thirty years ago, when I read the scriptures because the leaders of the Church counseled us to do so. That is, I did it out of a sense of duty. Do you know why I read the scriptures now?"

"Why *do* you read them, Bob?" he asked.

"Because they feed my soul. They fill me with light and understanding. Scripture reading is a significant part of my daily devotions and worship of God." I continued, "I think it's the same with attending church, paying tithing, doing home teaching, going to the temple, and carrying out all those other activities you mentioned. I do those things now because I enjoy them, because they teach and inspire me, because I love the Lord."

I'm suggesting that although I have miles to go before I rest (as far as my own spirituality is concerned), I can look back on my life and recognize that in many cases the works of righteousness have become more and more a part of me and less and less a set of responsibilities to be carried out.

Don't misunderstand me: There's nothing wrong with doing our Church assignments out of a sense of duty; being dutiful is something to be commended. Obedience is one of the first laws of heaven. But one of the glories of the gospel is that to the extent the Holy Spirit is allowed to work upon our soul—to educate our consciences and refine our feelings—we begin to do good works because that's just the way we are. They have become part of us. They evidence our discipleship and our loving covenant with the Savior.

Rule keeping is not a bad thing. At the same time, we must not be content with serving God wholly out of duty. Such an approach to life becomes laborious and can produce a kind of sterile legalism that results eventually in spiritual burnout. It is one thing to have *discipline* in our lives; it is quite another to have a *disposition* to love, serve, and carry out the will of the Father.

Thus, we pray for our hearts to be changed, to receive the spirit of our calling or assignment. We plead with God to purify our motives. We petition the heavens for divine strength and spiritual dynamism that are in no way self-generated; they represent a new life, a new life in Christ, a gracious gift from the Living God. The apostle Paul wrote that although he had died to the old ways of sin, yet he lived, but not by his own light and his own native strength and abilities: "Christ liveth in me" (Galatians 2:20).

Sometimes we can become so caught up with what people are *doing* that we pay little attention to what they are *becoming*. Elder Dallin H. Oaks taught that "the Final Judgment is not just an evaluation of a sum total of good and evil acts—what we have *done*. It is an acknowledgment of the final effect of our acts and thoughts—what we have *become*. It is not enough for anyone just to go through the motions. The commandments, ordinances, and covenants of the gospel are not a list of deposits required to be made in some heavenly account. The gospel of Jesus Christ is a plan that shows us how to become what our Heavenly

Father desires us to become" (Conference Report, October 2000, 41; emphasis in original).

Later in that same address, Elder Oaks continued: "We are challenged to move through a process of conversion toward that status and condition called eternal life. This is achieved not just by doing what is right, but by doing it for the right reason—for the pure love of Christ. . . . The reason charity never fails and the reason charity is greater than even the most significant acts of goodness . . . is that charity . . . is not an *act* but a *condition* or state of being" (Conference Report, October 2000, 43; emphasis in original).

True religion, real religion, the means by which we are literally linked with Deity, is a thing of the heart. It is manifest in good works, but it is borne of the Spirit, even "that Spirit which leadeth to do good—yea, to do justly, to walk humbly, to judge righteously" (D&C 11:12). Thus, Joseph Smith observed that "to be justified before God we must love one another: we must overcome evil; we must visit the fatherless and the widow in their affliction, and we must keep ourselves unspotted from the world [see James 1:27]: for *such virtues flow from the great fountain of pure religion,* strengthening our faith by adding every good quality that adorns the children of the blessed Jesus" (*Teachings of the Prophet Joseph Smith,* 76; emphasis added).

God's commandments are expressions of his love for us, his desire that we walk in paths of righteousness and that we abstain from the evils of a world that would destroy us, destroy our souls, and thereby rob us of happiness here and eternal reward hereafter. The faithful are promised "the good things of the earth." They are promised further that "they shall also be crowned with blessings from above, yea, and *with commandments not a few, and with revelations in their time*" (D&C 59:3–4; emphasis added).

We cannot keep a law of which we are ignorant. We cannot receive the blessings of obedience to a statute that has not been given to us. We cannot pursue a righteous path that has not been made known. Commandments are thus God's guidelines, his sacred structure by which we are assisted in our walk down that road that leads to life eternal. "For this is the love of God, that we keep his commandments: and his commandments are not grievous [oppressive, burdensome]" (1 John 5:3).

I thank the Lord for his guidance, for his chastening but ever-loving hand, for his willingness to work with us, for his patience as we mature in matters of faith.

FIFTEEN

"When He Falls
He Shall Rise Again"

THERE IS NOTHING MORE frustrating and confidence-eroding than sinning or making a mistake after we had assumed a particular action or disposition was well behind us. On such occasions we ask ourselves: "What is wrong with you? How could you do that? Wasn't this something you had put away for good? Do you think the Lord will keep forgiving this over and over again?" The pain of stepping momentarily and unexpectedly into the darkness after we have walked in the light is a miserable pain, a disgusting feeling.

Why do we do it? How can we make such progress, enjoy such freedom from sin, feel better and better about our relationship with God, and then in an unguarded moment step outside the bounds and find ourselves at the starting gate once again? I suppose such things happen because we are human. We're mortal. It's not generally because we want to err. The climb of spirituality is seldom a straight and steady movement up the mountain; it is, more likely than not, punctuated with detours and side canyons, wasted time and effort, slips and stumbles. That's because most of us grow gradually, not exponentially.

Luke 15 is a fascinating chapter. The chapter begins with Jesus being criticized for eating and drinking with "sinners." In response our Lord delivers three parables of lost things: the parable of the lost sheep, the parable of the lost coin, and the parable of the lost son, the latter known to most of us as the parable of the prodigal son. As he ends the first two parables, the Master Teacher utters these words: "Joy shall be in heaven over one sinner that repenteth, more than over ninety and nine just persons, which need no repentance" (v. 7).

What a startling comment! Who do you know that needs no repentance? How many mortals do you know who have never taken a backward step or a moral detour? As the Prophet Joseph explained concerning these parables, "There is joy in the presence of the angels of God over one sinner that repenteth, more than over ninety-and-nine just persons that are so righteous; they will be damned anyhow; you cannot save them" (*Teachings of the Prophet Joseph Smith*, 277–78). Jesus' words are clearly a rebuke and a denunciation of self-righteousness and pride. We all need repentance. We all have wandered and gone astray (Isaiah 53:6). We all seek forgiveness.

In Doctrine and Covenants 117 three men were given specific charges. William Marks, the president of the Kirtland Stake, and Newel K. Whitney, the bishop in Kirtland, were counseled to settle up their affairs and move to Missouri with the rest of the Saints. It appears that both of them were striving to acquire some extra cash from the sale of Kirtland properties, and this "littleness of soul" displeased the Lord (v. 11). "Let them repent of all their sins, and of all their covetous desires, before me, saith the Lord; for what is property unto me?" (v. 4).

The third person was Oliver Granger, the Prophet's agent or attorney-in-fact in Kirtland. "Oliver Granger was a very ordinary man," President Boyd K. Packer noted. "He was mostly blind having 'lost his sight by cold and exposure' (*History of the Church,* 4:408). The First Presidency described him as 'a man of the most strict integrity and moral virtue; and in fine, to be a man of God' (*History of the Church,* 3:350).

"When the Saints were driven from Kirtland, Ohio, in a scene that would be repeated in Independence, Far West, and in Nauvoo, Oliver was left behind to sell their properties for what little he could.

There was not much chance that he could succeed. And, really, he did not succeed!

"But the Lord said, 'Let him contend earnestly for the redemption of the First Presidency of my Church, saith the Lord; and when he falls he shall rise again, for his sacrifice shall be more sacred unto me than his increase, saith the Lord' (D&C 117:13).

"What did Oliver Granger do that his name should be held in sacred remembrance? Nothing much, really. *It was not so much what he did as what he was*" (*Ensign*, November 2004, 86; emphasis added).

The words of Doctrine and Covenants 117:13 fascinate me: "And *when he falls he shall rise again, for his sacrifice shall be more sacred unto me than his increase,* saith the Lord" (emphasis added). This passage is one that fills my soul with hope, with optimism, with excitement about the truth that the all-righteous and holy Being we worship will work with us, be patient with us, and offer us an opportunity to get up and dust ourselves off whenever we fall.

President Packer continued: "Some worry endlessly over missions that were missed, or marriages that did not turn out, or babies that did not arrive, or children that seem lost, or dreams unfulfilled, or because age limits what they can do. *I do not think it pleases the Lord when we worry because we think we never do enough or that what we do is never good enough.*

"Some needlessly carry a heavy burden of guilt which could be removed through confession and repentance.

"The Lord did not say of Oliver, '[*If*] he falls,' but '*When* he falls he shall rise again' (D&C 117:13; emphasis added)" (*Ensign,* November 2004, 87; emphasis added).

Character is not a product of a sinless life, not a result of never making a mistake or an error of judgment, but rather of never staying down when we have fallen. We show what we're made of and of our determination to follow the Christ by getting up and dusting ourselves off one more time than we fall. In so doing, we demonstrate our acceptance of the divine offer to us to regroup, rework, retrust, and recommit ourselves to the Christian life.

SIXTEEN

The Father's Down Payment

WHILE I WAS SERVING AS A BISHOP, a sister in our ward telephoned me to request that I visit her. She was dying of cancer and had chosen not to pursue chemotherapy. This sister was an absolutely wonderful woman, as Christlike as anyone I knew. She and her noble husband had served several full-time missions for the Church, and everyone in the ward looked to her as an example of spirituality. There was a quiet and sweet serenity in her countenance, and her voice reflected the love of Christ and her love for all of God's children. She indicated on the phone that her coming graduation into the next life was near at hand and asked if it would be possible for me to come to her home to conduct a temple recommend interview, because she was not able to get around anymore. She wanted to have a current recommend at the time of her passing. I told her I would be delighted to visit her and said that I would bring the stake president with me.

The stake president and I had a deeply moving experience with her in her home. The stake president listened as I asked the questions and as she responded. When the formal interview was completed, I asked her how she felt about death. She answered, to my surprise, "Oh, Bishop, I just don't know if I'm ready to go home. I worry that I haven't done enough!"

I was stunned. Here was a beautiful, celestial person, one who had served dutifully and faithfully for more than sixty years, had given herself to the Lord and his work, and had brought sunshine into the lives of thousands. And she was worried about facing death!

The problem was not the quality of this woman's life. She possessed a testimony of Jesus and of his gospel. She had a solid understanding of that gospel. She was active and involved in the Church. She had spent a lifetime serving others and doing her best to live a life befitting the call to discipleship.

But she was lacking in important ways, doctrinal ways: She did not understand that her life was in order, nor did she grasp how the Lord had accepted of her offerings. A lack of understanding, not a lack of goodness or faithfulness, prevented her from feeling that peace that passes all understanding (John 14:27;

Philippians 4:7), the peace that signals divine approbation.

Peace is what it's all about in the gospel sense. Although most members of the Church know what peace is, I believe peace has not yet been given its day; I feel that as a people we have not fully appreciated what a remarkable fruit of the Spirit (Galatians 5:22) and what a transcendent manifestation of the new birth peace is.

Peace is a priceless gift in a world that is at war with itself. Disciples look to him who is the Prince of Peace for their succor and their support. They know that peace is not only a cherished commodity in the here and now but also a harbinger of glorious things yet to be. Peace is a sure and solid sign from God that the heavens are pleased. As the Savior asked Oliver Cowdery, "Did I not speak peace to your mind concerning the matter? What greater witness can you have than from God?" (D&C 6:23).

Sin and neglect of duty result in disunity of the soul and strife and confusion; repentance and forgiveness and rebirth bring quiet and rest and peace. Sin results in disorder; the Holy Spirit brings order and congruence. The world and the worldly cannot bring peace; they cannot settle the soul (D&C 101:36). "Peace, peace to him that is far off, and to him that is near, saith the Lord; and I will heal him. But the wicked are like the troubled sea, when it cannot rest, whose waters cast up mire and dirt. There is no peace, saith my God, to the wicked" (Isaiah 57:19–20).

Hope in Christ, which is a natural result of our saving faith in Christ, comes through spiritual reawakening. We sense our place in the royal family and are warmed by the sweet family association. And what is our indication that we are on course? How do we know we are in the gospel harness? "Hereby know we that we dwell in him, and he in us, *because he hath given us of his Spirit*" (1 John 4:13; emphasis added). The presence of God's Spirit is the attestation, the divine assurance, that we are headed in the right direction. It is God's seal, his anointing, his unction (1 John 2:20) to us that our lives are in order.

I recall vividly the fear and awful anxiety that Shauna and I felt when we decided to purchase our first home. We had no money in savings, and although I had a steady job, it did not bring a great income. Yet we knew that we had to get started sometime if we ever hoped to become homeowners. We determined to start slowly. A dear friend of ours, a fellow seminary teacher, located a place for us in his neighborhood. Another friend offered to lend us the down payment. (Thank goodness for friends!) It was at this time that Shauna and I became acquainted with the concept of earnest money. We made a goodwill payment to the owner of the home, a small amount to be sure but sufficient to evidence our seriousness about purchasing the home. That amount was called the earnest money. It was a token payment, a gesture of our desire to acquire a home, a promissory note of sorts.

God works with us in similar ways. How does he communicate to us that we are following a proper course? He sends his Spirit. The Holy Ghost thus represents God's "earnest money" on us, his down payment, his goodwill gesture and assurance to us that he is serious about saving us and that one day he will own us and claim us fully as his. The apostle Paul wrote that the Saints had trusted in Christ, "after that ye heard the word of truth, the gospel of your salvation: in whom also after that ye believed, *ye were sealed with that holy Spirit of promise, which is the earnest of our inheritance until the redemption of the purchased possession,* unto the praise of his glory" (Ephesians 1:13–14; emphasis added; see also 2 Corinthians 1:21–22).

In short, the same Spirit that eventually seals us up unto eternal life places a seal of approval upon our lives here and now. Though the fulness of the blessings of eternal life is not available until the world to come, the peace and rest and hope that are harbingers of those unspeakable blessings can and should be ours in this world. President David O. McKay observed that "the gospel of Jesus Christ, as revealed to the Prophet Joseph Smith, is in very deed, in every way, the power of God unto salvation. It is salvation *here*—here and now. It gives to every man the perfect life, here and now, as well as hereafter" (*Gospel Ideals,* 6).

"Salvation is a big and comprehensive word," Christian author John Stott emphasized. "It embraces the totality of God's saving work, from beginning to end. In fact salvation has three tenses, past, present and future. . . . 'I have been saved (in the past) from the penalty of sin by a crucified Saviour. I am being saved (in the present) from the power of sin by a living Saviour. And I shall be saved (in the future) from the very presence of sin by a coming Saviour.' . . .

"If therefore you were to ask me, 'Are you saved?' there is only one correct biblical answer which I could give you: 'yes and no.' Yes, in the sense that by the sheer grace and mercy of God through the death of Jesus Christ my Saviour he has forgiven my sins, justified me and reconciled me to himself. But no, in the sense that I still have a fallen nature and live in a fallen world and have a corruptible body, and I am longing for my salvation to be brought to its triumphant completion" (*Authentic Christianity,* 168; see also Stott, *Why I Am a Christian,* 83).

There is, then, a sense in which we can know that we will be saved or exalted hereafter. If we are living in such a way that the Holy Ghost can dwell with us, then we are in covenant, on course, in Christ. If we are doing all we can to cultivate the gift and gifts of the Spirit, then we are living in what might be called a saved condition.

President Young declared, "*If we are saved, we are happy,* we are filled with light, glory, intelligence, and we pursue a course to enjoy the blessings that the Lord has in store for us. If we continue to pursue that course, it produces just the thing we want, that is, *to be saved at this present moment.* And this will lay the foundation to be saved for ever and for ever, which will amount to an eternal salvation" (*Journal of Discourses,* 1:131; emphasis added; see also 8:124–25).

We cannot overcome the world if we live in a constant state of spiritual insecurity. Satan, the arch deceiver, is versatile and observant. As surely as the day follows the night, he will strike at our sense of insecurity before God if we do not acquire that hope or assurance that comes by and through His Holy Spirit. We overcome the world through Christ—through being changed by Christ, captained by Christ, and consumed in Christ (Ezra Taft Benson, Conference Report, October 1985, 5–6).

We need not be possessed of an unholy or intemperate zeal in order to be saved; we need only be constant and dependable. God is the other party with us in the gospel covenant. He is the controlling partner. He lets us know, through the influence of the Spirit, that the gospel covenant is still intact and the supernal promises are sure. The Savior invites us to learn the timeless and comforting lesson that "he who doeth the works of righteousness shall receive his reward, even peace in this world, and eternal life in the world to come" (D&C 59:23). Peace. Hope. Assurance. These things come to us by virtue of the atoning blood of Jesus Christ and as a natural result of our new creation. They serve as an anchor to the soul, a solid and steady reminder of who we are and Whose we are.

SEVENTEEN

There Is No All at Once

WHEN WE COME UNTO CHRIST by covenant, the scriptures teach us, we are *justified*—we are made righteous, exonerated, pronounced innocent before God. That is, our legal standing before him has changed. We have moved from a fallen condition to a redeemed condition, from a state of alienation to a state of reconciliation and acceptance. I believe this is what Moroni meant when he spoke of coming unto Christ and being made *perfect* in him; we are perfect in the sense that we are made whole, fully formed, spiritually mature, finished (Moroni 10:32). God's pronouncement upon us that we are clean, free from sin, and right before him is an act of grace (D&C 20:30). Our sins are removed, and at the same time we have imputed to us (put on our account, if you will) the righteousness of God. It is indeed a great exchange (2 Corinthians 5:21).

We have been given the gift of the Holy Ghost, the right to the companionship of the third member of the Godhead. The Holy Ghost is a revelator, a comforter, a teacher, a discerner, and a sealer. He is also a sanctifier, the means by which we are cleansed by the blood of Christ, the medium by which filth and dross are burned out of our souls as though by fire; we thus refer to such cleansing and purification as the baptism by fire. We strive to keep the commandments and cultivate the gift and gifts of the Spirit in our lives thereafter, and through the years the sanctification process takes place. Sanctification is also an act of grace (D&C 20:31), a refining and renewing process that goes forward for the remainder of our days. Like Zion of old, the Saints of God become fully pure in heart "in process of time" (Moses 7:21).

"Yielding to the realities of our days," Elder Neal A. Maxwell wrote, "is actually part of spiritual submissiveness by recognizing a divine timetable in which 'all things must come to pass in their time' (D&C 64:32). When we pray 'Thy will be done,' our submission includes yielding to God's timing. He lives in a unique circumstance wherein the past, present, and future blend in an 'eternal now.' Those of us who need to wear mere wristwatches should be reluctant, therefore, to insist on our timetables for Him" (*Whom the Lord Loveth,* 18).

What would we think of a father who said to his fourteen-year-old son, "Larry, if you really love me, you will be tall. I have been short all my life. I love basketball and have always wanted to be a star forward on a successful team. But it's never worked out. If you love me, if you have any respect for me as your father, you will grow to be six foot eight."

Such a request would be cruel and unkind, especially given the fact that Larry has little control over how tall he will be. He can eat the right foods, train and work out, and do everything within his power to be big and strong, but he cannot control how tall he will be. In a way, it's just the same with spiritual growth. We cannot program it. We cannot specify and delineate and produce. We cannot prepare formulas and plans which will result in specific spiritual phenomena. We cannot say with certitude that if a man or woman does X and Y and Z, then a dream or vision will be forthcoming; that if he or she does A or B or C consistently, then he or she will be able to prophesy or speak in tongues. We can prepare the soil, if you will, we can provide a setting for development, but that is all. We must exercise patience and trust in the Lord and his purposes.

I knew one man who claimed that he would be perfect by the age of thirty. He set out on a deliberate program, organized his goals according to a ten-year, five-year, one-year, monthly, weekly, and daily plan. He pushed and pulled and stretched and reached spiritually, as much so as any person I have known. But he was not perfect at thirty. We cannot force spiritual things. A woman I am acquainted with announced to several friends that she would make her calling and election sure by the time she was fifty years old. She has been faithful in the Church. She has long since passed the age of fifty and is greatly discouraged because the goal of her existence, so far as she knows, has not been realized. We simply cannot force spiritual things.

Endless prayers, lengthy scripture vigils, excessive fasting—all of these, though at first well-intended, may come to be more a curse than a blessing. Gospel growth must come slowly, steadily, gradually. Elder Boyd K. Packer has warned: "Such words as *compel, coerce, constrain, pressure, demand* do not describe our privileges with the Spirit. You can no more force the Spirit to respond than you can force a bean to sprout, or an egg to hatch before its time. You can create a climate to foster growth; you can nourish, and protect; but you cannot force or compel: You must await the growth. Do not be impatient to gain great spiritual knowledge. Let it grow, help it grow; but do not force it, or you will open the way to be misled" *("That All May Be Edified,"* 338).

For years I wrestled with the meaning of the parable of the ten virgins, as recorded in Matthew 25. The scene seemed so wrong, the message so counter to all else that the Master taught. Why couldn't the wise virgins just break down and share their oil? If each one just contributed a little, I reasoned, perhaps everyone, or at least some of the "foolish" ones could make it to the wedding to meet the Bridegroom. An experience taught me the answer.

While I was serving as a priesthood leader, a husband and wife came to see me. They were both distressed about the state of their marriage and family; things seemed to be coming apart in their lives.

"How can I help?" I asked.

"We need more spirituality in our home," the wife answered.

I asked a few questions. "How often do you pray as a family?"

They answered that their schedules precluded any kind of family prayer.

"Do you hold family home evening?"

"Bill and I bowl on Monday nights" was the response.

"Do you ever take occasion to read the scriptures as a family or as individuals?"

The husband answered, "Reading hurts my eyes."

"Well, then, how can I help you?"

Again the reply: "We want the Spirit in our lives."

It was as though they were saying to me, "Brother Millet, could you reach down into your heart and your experiences and lend us five years of daily prayer, ten years of regular scripture study, and fifteen years of family spiritual activities?"

I realized dramatically that there are simply some things that we cannot share. I also came to appreciate that, like the small oil lamps of the Middle East that require a careful and methodical and slow effort to fill, so in our own lives we need to build our reservoirs of faith and spiritual experience gradually and consistently. Consistent gospel growth—that was the answer.

President Spencer W. Kimball taught: "The foolish asked the others to share their oil, but spiritual preparedness cannot be shared in an instant. . . . This was not selfishness or unkindness. The kind of oil that is needed to illuminate the way and light up the darkness is not shareable. . . . In our lives the oil of preparedness is accumulated drop by drop in righteous living" (*Faith Precedes the Miracle*, 255–56).

Finally, in our eagerness to prepare and do all that

is required, we must be careful that our personal expectations, though rigorous, are realistic. Except for a few cases that are so miraculous they are written up in scripture, being born again is a process; we are born again gradually, from one level of spiritual grace to a higher one. Almost always people are sanctified—made clean and holy and pure through the blood of Christ by the medium of the Holy Ghost—in gradual, line-upon-line fashion. Thus, ultimate perfection and salvation are processes. Let me repeat: One of the great challenges we face in our quest for spiritual maturity is to balance a type of divine discontent, a constant yearning for improvement and growth, with what Nephi called a "perfect brightness of hope" (2 Nephi 31:20), the assurance born of the Spirit that although we are not perfect—we have much sanctification and perfection ahead of us—we have a hope in Christ, a quiet confidence that in and through him we will in time overcome all things and go on to eternal life.

We are called to work out our salvation with fear and trembling before God (Philippians 2:12; Alma 34:37). This injunction is in no way intended to convey the idea that we can do it ourselves, that we should become caught up in a kind of works-righteousness. Rather, the phrase connotes that salvation is in fact a process of learning line upon line, precept upon precept. It is a divine labor in which we allow the Lord to work in us, empower us, motivate us, and purify us over time (Philippians 2:13). God and I are working together to save my soul.

One of my favorite scriptures comes from Paul's first letter to the Corinthians. Paul acknowledged to the Saints in Corinth that when he visited them he "came not with excellency of speech or of wisdom" but rather he "determined not to know any thing among [them], save Jesus Christ, and him crucified." In sweet humility this learned and impressive orator then added this treasure: "But as it is written, Eye hath not seen, nor ear heard, neither have entered into the heart of man, the things which God hath prepared for them that love him" (1 Corinthians 2:1–2, 9).

That expression is a comforting assurance to each and every one of us, a reminder that although there are moments of intense joy and peace in this world, the glories and feelings and transcendent associations of a future world are even grander. As powerful and encouraging as these thoughts are, they are not Paul's property alone: They were spoken first by Isaiah, and, incidentally, in a slightly different manner. "For since the beginning of the world," Isaiah declared, "men have not heard, nor perceived by the ear, neither hath the eye seen, O God, beside thee, what he hath prepared *for him that waiteth for him*" (Isaiah 64:4; emphasis added; compare D&C 133:45). To wait on the Lord is closely related to having *hope* in the Lord. Waiting on and hoping in the Lord are scriptural words that focus not on frail and faltering mortals but on a sovereign and omni-loving God, who fulfills his promises to the people of promise in his own time.

Hope is more than worldly wishing. It is expectation, anticipation, assurance. We wait on the Lord because we have hope in him. "For we through the Spirit wait for the hope of righteousness by faith" (Galatians 5:5). Thus we wait on the Lord, not in the sense that we sit and wring our hands and glance at our clocks compulsively, but rather in that we exercise patience in his providential hand, knowing full well, by the power of the Holy Spirit, that the Father of Lights will soon transform a darkened world, all in preparation for the personal ministry of the Light of the World (1 Corinthians 1:4–8).

To be impatient with God is to lose sight of the truth—and thus require regular reminders—that our Heavenly Father loves us, is mindful of our present problems and daily dilemmas, and has a plan, both cosmic and personal, for our happiness here and our eternal reward hereafter. To wait on him, on the other hand, is to be "confident of this very thing, that he which hath begun a good work in you will perform it until the day of [the coming of] Jesus Christ" (Philippians 1:6). That is, to wait on the Lord is to exercise a lively hope that the God who is in his heaven is also working upon and through his people on earth.

Indeed, the glorious assurance, particularly to us who live in the midst of crime and indecency, is this: "Hast thou not known? hast thou not heard, that *the everlasting God, the Lord, the Creator of the ends of the earth, fainteth not, neither is weary?* there is no searching of his understanding. *He giveth power to the faint; and to them that have no might he increaseth strength.* Even the youths shall faint and be weary, and the young men shall utterly fall: but *they that wait upon the Lord shall renew their strength;* they shall mount up with wings as eagles; they shall run, and not be weary; and they shall walk, and not faint" (Isaiah 40:28–31; emphasis added). Some things are simply worth waiting for.

EIGHTEEN

Why Should God Let Me into Heaven?

THOSE WHO HAVE COME UNTO Christ by covenant are entitled to an optimism borne not alone of positive thinking but of the joyous promises set forth in the doctrines of salvation. "True doctrine, understood, changes attitudes and behavior," Elder Boyd K. Packer taught us (Conference Report, October 1986, 20).

Those who have enjoyed the love of God in their life—particularly that pure love of Christ extended through the merciful atoning sacrifice of our Lord and Savior—have reason to rejoice. Indeed, the atonement of Jesus Christ is foundational to everything. There is no forgiveness, no healing, no happiness or feelings of worth, no eternal perspective, no power to continue on the strait and narrow, no resurrection from the dead, no glorification hereafter, no purpose to it all without the Atonement. And undergirding that atonement are three vital attributes of Deity:

1. *His love.* God loves us, so he sent his Beloved Son into the world to ransom us from sin and death and hell and endless torment (John 3:16; D&C 34:3). Jesus, the Good Shepherd, condescended to perform a search-and-rescue mission, to retrieve those who are lost and to return them to the fold.

2. *His righteousness.* One of the great ironies of life, as set forth in scripture, is that in the long run we are saved by the goodness and perfection of our Blessed Savior. "I know that thou art redeemed," Lehi said to his son Jacob, "because of the righteousness of thy Redeemer" (2 Nephi 2:3). Our Father takes away the guilt from our hearts as we repent "through the merits of his Son" (Alma 24:10; compare Helaman 14:11–12).

3. *His mercy and grace.* To receive mercy is to acquire the divine assurance that we will *not* receive hereafter what we deserve (eternal punishment). To receive grace is to acquire the divine assurance that we *will* receive hereafter what we do not deserve (eternal life). These supernal blessings flow to us as a result of our faith in the Lord Jesus Christ. To the extent that ours is a total trust in him, a complete confidence in him, and a ready reliance upon him, we gain the hope in Christ that serves as the anchor to the soul (Hebrews 6:19; Ether 12:4). We gain the anticipation,

expectation, and assurance that through him and because of him we're going to make it to our destination. We may not be there yet, but we're getting there, a small stretch at a time.

A short time ago a colleague and I sat at lunch with two prominent theologians. This was not our first visit together, as we had met two years earlier and had had a sweet and delightful discussion of Jesus Christ, the centrality of his atonement, the lifting and liberating powers of his grace, and how our discipleship is and should be lived out day by day. In our meetings there was no defensiveness, no pretense, no effort to put the other down or prove him wrong. Instead, there was a simple exchange of views, an acknowledgment of our differences, and a spirit of rejoicing in the central features of the doctrine of Christ about which we were in complete agreement—a sobering spirit of gratitude for the incomparable blessings that flow from the life and death and transforming power of the Redeemer.

Now, two years later, we picked up where we had left off, almost as if no time had passed at all. Toward the end of our meeting, one friend turned to me and said, "Okay, Bob, here's the question of questions, the one thing I would like to ask in order to determine what you really believe." I indicated that I thought I was ready for his query, though I readily admit that his preface to the question was a bit unnerving. He continued: "You are standing before the judgment bar of the Almighty, and God turns to you and asks: 'Robert Millet, what right do you have to enter heaven? Why should I let you in?'" It was not the kind of question I had anticipated. (I had expected something more theologically theoretical. This question was theological, to be sure, but it was poignant, practical, penetrating, and personal.) For about thirty seconds I tried my best to envision such a scene, searched my soul, and sought to be as clear and candid as possible.

Before I indicate exactly what I said, let us go forward twenty-four hours in time to a conference of LDS single adults from throughout New England. I was to speak to the group on the topic "Hope in Christ." Two-thirds of the way through the address, I felt it appropriate to share the experience from the day before. I posed to the young people the same question that had been posed to me.

There was a noticeable silence in the room, an evidence of quiet contemplation. After allowing the audience to think about the question for a minute or so, I walked up to a young woman on the front row and said, "How would I respond? Would I say to the Lord something like, 'Well, I should go to heaven because I was baptized into the Church, I served a full-time mission, I married in the temple, I attend worship services regularly, I read my scriptures daily, I pray in the morning and at night . . . '"

At that point the young woman cut me off with, "Wait . . . wait . . . I don't feel right about your answer. In fact, it makes me very uncomfortable."

"Why would it make you uncomfortable?" I responded. "I've done all those things, haven't I? Shouldn't I provide the Lord a list of my good deeds?"

She wisely answered, "I think he knows what you've done with your life. Your answer sounds like you're reading God your resume."

"You're right," I said. "I could never feel comfortable standing before an all-wise, all-righteous God, gloating over or even just detailing my earthly accomplishments. So what do we say?"

Several hands went up. One young man blurted out, "How did you answer? Tell us what you said!"

I thought back upon the previous day, recalled many of the feelings that had swirled in my heart at the time, and told the audience how I had answered:

"I looked my friend in the eye and replied, 'I would say to God, I claim the right to enter heaven because of my complete trust in the Lord Jesus Christ and my reliance upon his merits and mercy and grace.'"

The silence of my young listeners and the nodding of heads confirmed the assessment of my questioner from the day before: "That's the correct answer."

Clearly, good works matter. They are important as an indicator of what we are becoming through the powers of Jesus Christ; they manifest who and what we are. Faith cannot be separated from acts of faithfulness. Coming unto Christ cannot be divorced from dedicated discipleship. But we also know that there will never be enough good deeds on our part—prayers, hymns, charitable acts, financial contributions, or thousands of hours of Church service—to save ourselves, to *earn* eternal life.

The work of salvation requires the work of God. Unaided man is and will forevermore be lost, fallen, and unsaved. It is only in the strength of the Lord that we are able to face life's challenges, handle life's dilemmas, engage life's contradictions, endure life's trials, and eventually defeat life's inevitable foe—death.

Again, I cannot imagine myself standing before the purest Being in the universe, the all-wise and all-loving and all-knowing Creator of heaven and earth, speaking of my own accomplishments, displaying my mortal medals, or reading my impressive press clippings. Such would be so very inappropriate, so out of place, so absolutely foreign to the moment. We labor here to perform the works of righteousness, not that we may one day wave them before the Almighty and seek thereby to capture his approval, but rather to become people of purpose, people who show our love for God by serving our fellow man (Matthew 25:40; Mosiah 2:17), people whose hearts have been transformed by participation in the realm of divine experience. Let's repeat ourselves one final time: Grace represents God's acceptance of me. Faith represents my acceptance of God's acceptance of me. Peace is my acceptance of me.

On that sacred occasion when we stand before God to give an accounting of what we have done with our lives, it will feel ever so much more comfortable and right and good to have allowed our Advocate, the Chosen One, to have pleaded before the face of the Father in our behalf (D&C 45:3–5; Moses 7:39). My soul resonates to the words of Nephi: "O Lord, I have trusted in thee, and I will trust in thee forever. I will not put my trust in the arm of flesh. . . . Therefore I will lift up my voice unto thee; yea, I will cry unto thee, my God, the rock of my righteousness" (2 Nephi 4:34–35). And I have a feeling that heaven holds a place for those whose lives have come to reflect that kind of loving reliance. That's where I want to be.

***

I sat with a young man once who had spent the past three years of his life wrestling mightily with drug addictions. He had become involved in many serious, soul-destroying activities during that time and had lost all hope in Christ, had left the Church, and had just about given up on life. As I sought to encourage him, to testify that there is a way back and that he had not sinned away his opportunity for peace here and salvation hereafter, he muttered through his tears: "But the way is so far back. It will take me so long to make it back."

I felt a flash of inspiration in that moment and replied, "How long it takes is totally in your hands. It depends entirely on how tenaciously and consistently you pursue the path of repentance."

Here was a young man who, looking at the distance to travel back to the path of peace, would have been somewhat justified in saying, "You can't get there from here" or "I can never get there" or "The journey is too long!" That expression is completely true. That is, it's true if he chooses to try to get there without assistance. He could not, worlds without end, forgive his own sins, cleanse his own heart, motivate or empower himself to continue in the upward climb, or find peace through his own unaided efforts. But getting there was doable if he chose to open himself to the powers of heaven and receive the heavenly gift.

We go to church, serve others, search the scriptures, fast and pray, participate in the ordinances of the temple, all in an effort to bridge the chasm between us and the heavens, to gain fellowship with our Heavenly Father and his Son Jesus Christ (1 John 1:3). We teach and we listen, we minister and we receive counsel, we serve long hours in our callings and assignments, all to the end that we might grow up in the Lord and eventually receive a fulness of the Holy Ghost (D&C 109:15).

It is a long path, a strait path, a mountainous path that winds and curls and ascends, a journey that requires faith and energy and perseverance to reach the top. There are intermediate stops along the way, summits and plateaus that provide temporary rest and reassurance. But climbers will not find real satisfaction unless they are pressing toward the top of the mountain. Elder Bruce R. McConkie said, "If we die in the faith, that is the same thing as saying that *our calling and election has been made sure* and that we will go on to eternal reward hereafter" (funeral address, 5; emphasis added).

Further, I believe it is not only wise but vital that

we ponder frequently upon the truth that we *have* come unto Christ; we *have* accepted him and his gospel; we *have* enjoyed the fruits of his redeeming blood; we *have* become members of the household of faith, the body of Christ; and we *have* received the promise of eternal life as we remain on the gospel path (D&C 6:13; 14:7; 50:5). Elder McConkie observed, "I think the Latter-day Saints have a great obligation pressing in upon them to rejoice in the Lord, to praise him for his goodness and grace, to ponder his eternal truths in their hearts" (Conference Report, October 1973, 55).

We're called to become a righteous people. How can we become righteous if we find ourselves making mistakes and committing sins? In the biblical languages, the word translated as *sin* implies iniquity, wrongful intent, breaking the commandments, and rebellion. It implies—and this is the point—"missing the mark," as we would if we were shooting arrows at a bull's-eye. A *righteous* man or woman is one "whose aim is true." Thus, righteousness is not some static goal to be attained in some distant day but rather a kind of "target practice. Whether my arrow finds its mark or falls a hundred feet away, the daily practice of [righteousness] is how I improve my aim. I will continue to sin, no doubt about it, but that is not my aim. My true aim is to live as God wants me to live" (Taylor, *Speaking of Sin,* 48–49, 101).

If we're striving toward a righteous life, we're on our way. We're headed in the right direction. We slip and fall now and then, but we get up and keep moving with our Lord's divine assistance. The Master beckoned us at the Last Supper, "Let not your heart be troubled, neither let it be afraid" (John 14:2).

Elder Jeffrey R. Holland, in speaking of those tender words, observed: "That may be one of the Savior's commandments that is, even in the hearts of otherwise faithful Latter-day Saints, *almost universally disobeyed;* and yet I wonder whether our resistance to this invitation could be any more grievous to the Lord's merciful heart. I can tell you this as a parent: as concerned as I would be if somewhere in their lives one of my children were seriously troubled or unhappy or disobedient, nevertheless I would be infinitely more devastated if I felt that at such a time that child could not trust me to help or thought his or her interest was unimportant to me or unsafe in my care. In that same spirit, I am convinced that none of us can appreciate *how deeply it wounds the loving heart of the Savior of the world* when He finds that His people do not feel confident in His care or secure in His hands or trust in His commandments" (*Trusting Jesus,* 68; emphasis added).

I rejoice in the knowledge that has come to me that God our Father lives: He hears our prayers, knows our names, sees our challenges, knows our hearts, intervenes and orchestrates events in our lives, and loves us perfectly. I am eternally grateful to know that Jesus is the Christ, the Promised Messiah, the Son of the living God: He lived a perfect life; taught his gospel clearly and powerfully; performed miracles, such as feeding the multitudes, healing the sick, causing the blind to see and the deaf to hear, and even raising people from the dead; he suffered and bled and died for our sins in Gethsemane and on Golgotha; and he rose from the dead, becoming "the firstfruits of them that slept." Because he rose from the dead, each of us will do the same (1 Corinthians 15:20–22).

Life and love and learning are forever. President Thomas S. Monson stated powerfully: "The passage of time has not altered the capacity of the Redeemer to change men's lives. As He said to the dead Lazarus, so He says to you and to me, 'Come forth' (John 11:43). I add: Come forth from the despair of doubt. Come forth from the sorrow of sin. Come forth from the death of disbelief. Come forth to a newness of life" (*Ensign,* November 2004, 58).

I know—by the same Spirit that whispers to my soul of the living reality of God and his Beloved Son—

that the gospel of Jesus Christ has been restored in our day, that Joseph Smith was called of God, that divine authority and sacred truths have been delivered to earth through him, that the keys of the kingdom of God have continued in rightful, uninterrupted succession from Joseph Smith to the present time.

I find great solace in the assurance that God is in our corner, is pulling for us, will save all who will be saved. His tender arm of mercy is extended all the day long. Eternal life is available to all. I am persuaded, with Paul, that "now is our salvation nearer than when we [first] believed" (Romans 13:11). The glories promised to the faithful hereafter are not reserved for the apostles and prophets but are just as available to you and me.

Are we there yet? For most of us, not quite. But we're on the path. We're on our way home to the waiting Father.

Sources

Conference Reports of The Church of Jesus Christ of Latter-day Saints. Salt Lake City: The Church of Jesus Christ of Latter-day Saints, April 1970, October 1973, October 1976, October 1985, October 1986, October 1994, October 1995, October 2000, April 2004.

Dew, Sheri. *No One Can Take Your Place.* Salt Lake City: Deseret Book, 2004.

Hinckley, Gordon B. *Teachings of Gordon B. Hinckley.* Salt Lake City: Deseret Book, 1997.

Holland, Jeffrey R. *Trusting Jesus.* Salt Lake City: Deseret Book, 2003.

Journal of Discourses. 26 vols. London: Latter-day Saints' Book Depot, 1854–86.

Kimball, Spencer W. *Faith Precedes the Miracle.* Salt Lake City: Deseret Book, 1974.

Lee, Harold B. *Stand Ye in Holy Places.* Salt Lake City: Deseret Book, 1974.

Lewis, C. S. *Mere Christianity.* New York: Touchstone, 1996.

Lucado, Max. *Just like Jesus.* Dallas, Tex.: W Publishing Group, 2003.

Lund, Gerald N. *Jesus Christ, Key to the Plan of Salvation.* Salt Lake City: Deseret Book, 1991.

Maxwell, Neal A. *The Neal A. Maxwell Quote Book.* Ed. Cory H. Maxwell. Salt Lake City: Bookcraft, 1997.

———. *Whom the Lord Loveth: The Journey of Discipleship.* Salt Lake City: Deseret Book, 2003.

McConkie, Bruce R. Address at the funeral service for Elder S. Dilworth Young, 13 July 1981, typescript.

———. *Doctrines of the Restoration: Sermons and Writings of Bruce R. McConkie.* Ed. Mark L. McConkie. Salt Lake City: Bookcraft, 1989.

———. "Jesus Christ and Him Crucified." *Speeches of the Year, 1976.* Provo, Utah: Brigham Young University Press, 1977.

———. "The Seven Deadly Heresies." *Speeches of the Year, 1980.* Provo, Utah: Brigham Young University Publications, 1981.

McKay, David O. *Gospel Ideals.* Salt Lake City: Improvement Era, 1953.

"Messages of Inspiration from President Hinckley." *Church News,* 31 August 2002.

Monson, Thomas S. *Ensign,* November 2004.

Nelson, Russell M. *The Power within Us.* Salt Lake City: Deseret Book, 1988.

Nibley, Hugh. *Temples of the Ancient World.* Ed. Donald W. Parry. Salt Lake City: Deseret Book and Foundation for Ancient Research and Mormon Studies (FARMS), 1994.

Packer, Boyd K. *Ensign,* November 2004.

———. *"That All May Be Edified."* Salt Lake City: Bookcraft, 1982.

———. "The Fountain of Life." Brigham Young University Fireside Address, 29 March 1992.

Richards, Stephen L. *Where Is Wisdom?* Salt Lake City: Deseret Book, 1955.

Sheldon, Charles. *In His Steps.* Grand Rapids: Spire Books, 1984.

Smith, Joseph. *History of The Church of Jesus Christ of Latter-day Saints.* Ed. B. H. Roberts. 2d ed. rev. 7 vols. Salt Lake City: The Church of Jesus Christ of Latter-day Saints, 1932–51.

———. *Lectures on Faith.* Salt Lake City: Deseret Book, 1985.

———. *Teachings of the Prophet Joseph Smith.* Sel. Joseph Fielding Smith. Salt Lake City: Deseret Book, 1976.

Smith, Joseph F. *Gospel Doctrine.* Salt Lake City: Deseret Book, 1971.

Stackhouse, John G., Jr. *Humble Apologetics: Defending the Faith Today.* New York: Oxford University Press, 2002.

Stanley, Andy. *How Good Is Good Enough?* Sisters, Oreg.: Multnomah Publishers, 2003.

Stott, John. *Authentic Christianity.* Ed. Timothy Dudley-Smith. Downers Grove, Ill.: InterVarsity Press, 1995.

———. *Why I Am a Christian.* Downers Grove, Ill.: InterVarsity Press, 2003.

Talmage, James E. *The House of the Lord.* Salt Lake City: Deseret Book, 1968.

Taylor, Barbara Brown. *Speaking of Sin: The Lost Language of Salvation.* Cambridge, Mass.: Cowley Publications, 2000.

Index